The adventures of a

Southern

~~Baptis~~✝

Buddhist

Pamela McConnell, MSW, LCSW

1

The Adventures of a Southern (Baptist) Buddhist

Pamela McConnell, MSW, LCSW

Published by Pamela McConnell, MSW, LCSW, 2022.

While every precaution has been taken in the preparation of this book, the publisher assumes no responsibility for errors or omissions, or for damages resulting from the use of the information contained herein.

THE ADVENTURES OF A SOUTHERN (BAPTIST) BUDDHIST

First edition. September 23, 2022.

Written by Pamela McConnell, MSW, LCSW.

Table of Contents

To my lovely son **Clint** and all his children, my Grands.

To all my mothers of the three times; and especially my present one: **Rheta.**

To all the boys I've loved before.

To all the places that shaped me; and especially my Pilgrimage places.

To all sentient beings of the three times: May they all be free.

To my Root Guru, **Venerable Geshla Kelsang Gyatso Rinpoche**; all the Buddhas of the 10 directions; and my Highest Yoga Tantra deity: female **Buddha Vajrayogini**. May I become just like you!

1. Gimme that Old Time Religion

I am Pam, born from parents from the DEEP South. As many from Appalachia (pronounced *Ap puh* **latch** *uh,* in those parts*)* moved north for work after The Great Depression, so did they transplant for a time.

My older brother, let's call him Saint (synonymous with Sanctimonious), was born in a holler before they left. Mom (and dad had something to do with it) got pregnant with him before they were married. That was fascinating to me, especially because they raised us strictly in a Holiness (Fundamentalist or Evangelical) church.

Mom said, "We weren't 'saved' then."

However; being saved, having religion or coming from a strict Christian family did NOT stop Saint or his younger siblings from having sex before they were married.

Baby brother Nate was born several years after his siblings. I observed him in his little red terrycloth, onesy Santa-suit with a matching cap. It had a white pompom on the end. Mom had just brought him home from the hospital and he was lying on the couch.

Upon examination, I became horrified, and went running into the kitchen to inform mom:

"He doesn't have any teeth!" I thought he was deformed.

Another time, out of curiosity, I punched him with my little fist to see if I could make him cry. Cry he did. I immediately felt guilty and sorrowful. I grabbed my Mr. Potato Head and bestowed it hurriedly on Nate. I loved Mr. Potato Head, but knew I must sacrifice it for my SIN.

I remembered this when Nate was tramping down the basement stairs and the dog tripped him. He fell, hitting his head, and was knocked unconscious. Saint was sent out to the garage to get dad and we all said a prayer. We were so grateful when Nate woke up.

Our basement was a scary place, especially when you were alone. It was fun roller skating around the big furnace with Saint and our cousins, but we were terrified when the only bathroom was in use and we had to use the spare toilet in the basement, alone.

We would holler up to mom: "Mom! Mom?"

She'd finally say, "What?"

We would say, "I like you and love you, Mom, OK? **OK**??"

She'd finally answer, "Ok."

We were reassured by her voice, but she was annoyed at being asked the same thing over and over, sweet as it was.

———◦———

I WAS BORN ON A SUNDAY and attended my first (of many) church services that Wednesday. My first memory was gazing up at a bright globe of light, mesmerized. It was a church light and I was a babe in mom's arms.

At the end of many sermons, our beloved pastor would give an altar call. Many would go down to the altar (a bench that one knelt before and prayed). I remember it sounded like a loud beehive: the sounds of many praying out loud; crying, shouting, and whispering all over the church.

I would look around, noting the distress and fervor on the parishioner's faces. At that point, no one was paying any attention to us kids. It seemed endless. Toward the end, someone might 'feel the spirit' and start jumping around or even running up and down the aisles, shouting joyfully:

"Hallelujah!"

"Thank you, Jesus!"

After that, folks would be called to stand up and testify about what God had done for them. The standard testimony for us kids was:

"I love Jesus with all my heart and I want to go all the way with him."

We were 'saved' after confessing our sins and letting Jesus into our hearts as our Savior.

There was another, higher level, called being 'sanctified.' That was when the Holy Spirit entered you. I was saved at about five years old; sanctified at about nine. I felt full of the love of Jesus and began reading The Bible and praying.

I sang the hymns with joy and could feel the loving worship vibe strongly. I usually listened intently to sermons, but Saint and I got a spanking once from dad, when we got home.

We were both trying to place our elbow on the armrest between us. I knocked his arm off, he knocked mine off; we pushed against each other with force, like we were arm wrestling.

Because the church denomination liked the saved to be baptized in moving water, I was baptized at 15 in a river in the South. Later, I would choose NOT to have my only child 'christened' at birth.

By the time I left home, I felt completely saturated with Christian teachings and promptly quit going to church. I was seeing things and feeling a dissonance that didn't make sense to me. I quit religion for well over a decade.

I estimated once that I'd heard ~3333 hours of preachin' during my childhood. That included: Sunday school, Sunday nights, Wednesday prayer meetings, vacation bible school, and revivals (during which the evangelists preached 'Hell Far 'n' Brimstone').

My family was very close to that first church family, which included Uncle Bob and his family. The parishioners took the place of family and friends, for the most part.

Uncle Bob and Aunt Betty had a gaggle of kids, the youngest three of whom played almost weekly with me, Saint and Nate. The two brothers were close and the families shared many holidays and their traditional after-Sunday-night-church tuna sandwiches and pop. The Pepsi came in bottles stored in wooden crates in those days.

Our cousins believed in 'Santy Claus', looking him up in the encyclopedia for proof. Uncle Bob always gave us Santa stockings filled with little goodies. Saint and I had been told the truth, our parents didn't believe in lies:

"*Thou shalt not bear false witness,*" was one of the 10 Commandments.

I told mom: "I WANT to believe in Santa!"

So I decided in my heart to believe in Santa. Much to my parents' chagrin, I had a mind of my own. A good mind. I learned to trust it. I gave myself the right to make my own decisions; whether they were based on reason, science or a strong feeling.

We cousins played many board games. Later in the South we would play cards, but never with a deck such as was used for poker. That deck of cards was seen as SINFUL. The two bothers were VERY competitive, and we kids learned cutthroat skills which crippled us in some ways later.

My favorite cousin was Bobbie. We were only a few months apart, but Uncle Bob made a big deal about getting her into school early. He didn't do her any favors. Bobbie was always emotionally immature and that may have been the first reason she later became a 'no count,' shiftless, druggie and thief.

In those early days we were very close, confiding in each other and doing normal little kid things like playing doctor behind the couch. She was always cute and funny and loved to flirt suggestively with the boys when she got to her teens. Her main motivation throughout life seemed to be—just have fun in the moment. She loved 'acting a fool,' that's how she got attention.

Our fathers worked at farming factories, making things like Farmall and John Deere tractors. Although we all lived in the suburbs near the Mississippi River, I remember still: mile after mile of corn fields, as far as the eye could see. The North was flat with black dirt and straight roads, while the southern mountains were very steep with curvy roads and red dirt.

Corn was the view, as the two families all took the trip every summer, back to the brothers' beloved mountains in the DEEP South. We stayed with both sets of grandparents. We kids usually slept on the floor with feather beds that made me sneeze. Mom's parents still had an outhouse in those days, with actual Sears & Roebuck catalogs to wipe with.

Mom told a story about how after she got saved, "I was 'convicted' about wearing make-up and jewelry. Because of that, I threw my wedding band down in the outhouse potty. Your dad fished it out and wouldn't give it back to me until decades later!"

I inherited that band several years after dad died, and still wear it today, but I've promised to pass it along to my niece.

All the school kids walked to school in the morning, home for lunch, back to school, home again: that was rain or shine and through several blizzards. Later in the southern mountains we would ride the school bus after walking half a mile to the end of the dirt road, carrying an armload of books and a trombone. School was often cut short, delayed or canceled entirely for snowy days in the South.

The old school I first went to looked like a brick mansion and had beautifully curved, polished wood railings on the double stairs and landings. During fire drills, the enclosed slides were used. They were thrilling and scary. A young child would have to slide down behind an older child. If you didn't keep your knee in, it would get skinned. It was that steep.

I enjoyed that first decade; being happy, innocent and joyful. I played with my friends in the suburb, at school and at church. I fit right in with all the other little white boys and girls. The girls all wore dresses to church and school. The only time I remembered feeling out of place was when mom sent a note to my teacher, forbidding me to participate in square dancing. It was so much fun. I never understood why it was a SIN.

Reading was a favorite pastime. I would read ahead in the Dick/Jane/Sally series, keeping a finger at the place where the rest of the class was reading. By 2nd grade I was reading Nancy Drew books to mom while she cooked. We bought the cheap mystery books at the new K-Mart and would then go through the drive-through of McDonald's; or let the carhop on skates wait on us in our car, at the A&W root beer stand.

I estimated once that I had read maybe 10,000 books. I would read into the night by the street light outside the bedroom window. I read The Bible three times. Mom had to force me to go out and play with my playmates at times. I began writing in diaries regularly, but ended up burning them when my first husband read them and held them against me.

The neighborhood kids would roller skate (old-timey skates that went over your shoes, with a roller skate key to adjust) around the block. We played ball and rode bikes in the alley and around the block. Mom wouldn't let me go to the park and play ball with Saint and the boys, saying it wasn't 'fitting.'

Saint and I were close in those days, being just a year apart. We looked a lot alike and were about the same size before he hit puberty. We especially looked alike when mom made us matching dress and shirt, out of the same cloth. He was protective of me, walking me to school the first few days. We played, fought, and shared secrets; as young children do. We always got a spanking from mom together, as we would each blame the other:

"He started it."

"No-SHE started it."

There was a little old lady who dressed all in black and was often on the sidewalk with her broom. All the kids thought she was a witch and teased her. She would threaten them with her broom and they would ride away. I would stop my bike and try to talk with the lady. She was probably a foreigner, because it was difficult to understand her.

However, she would smile at me. I was always intrigued by all kinds of people, especially those that were different.

Mom told a story about another 'crazy' lady who had, most likely, a mental disease (perhaps dementia). She would yell garbled words at her neighbors.

Mom said, "I looked out the window one day and saw little Pammy facing off with the crazy neighbor lady. You were 'talking' loudly to each other, wagging your fingers at each other!"

I wore dresses to my knees. I was not allowed to wear mini skirts when the Beatles became popular and everything changed. Later on there was no make-up or jewelry allowed, and my hair was not cut until I was in puberty. I knew to mind my mom, or else. I knew very well the biblical command:

"Honor thy father and thy mother."

Later after puberty I learned to roll up the waistband of my skirts to make them shorter, and to hide make-up and jewelry. I also hid hickies I got from boys; and the sunburn all over my body, from wearing the bikini hidden at the bottom of my underwear drawer.

I was blissfully unaware. It was easy when all the other girls at school and church looked much the same. Most of the church people did not have televisions—which were seen as Sinful. Because of this, more than a decade of the tv culture was a blank in future years. I never saw the moon landing, nor the footage of JFK's assassination, until much later.

However, the upright radio was always tuned to WDLM, Moody Radio of the Quad Cities. It was a religious station and mom listened while she did her household chores. She kneeled in their bedroom to prayer sometimes, and would often seem far away, staring into space.

When dad came home from work, he'd sometimes play records: Hank Williams, bluegrass, and military marches. He'd often bring home half a dozen comic books on the weekend.

I read and played and took piano lessons and was happy. I loved school and church. I never felt like I HAD to have a tv, or cable or HBO to be happy. In retrospect, it was an ideal childhood in some ways. My loving foundation caused me to be strong and resilient for all that would follow. Everything was "hunkydory," as dad used to say. I didn't know the difference.

One of the few anxious or painful times was when I developed impetigo from infected mosquito bites. I always had itchy skin and couldn't refrain from scratching. Mom took me to the doctor and they gave her silver nitrate cream which tinted my skin grayish black for some time.

———————◉———————

IT WASN'T UNTIL I WAS in my teens or twenties that I would remember first being molested at four by Grandpa Claude (but let's call him Chester; rhymes with molester), who had come for a visit up north. He had offered to sit with me while mom walked to the bank in the snow (she hadn't learned to drive yet). Saint was at kindergarten and dad was working.

Chester had little Pam sit in his lap. He began rubbing outside and then inside her little panties. She was very still, not understanding what was happening. He spit on his fingers and began rubbing inside. That was disgusting for little Pam, who had been taught that spitting on others is wrong. She got plain mad that he spit on her and jumped off his lap. She got between the old upright radio and the corner of the wall, hiding with her face turned to the wall. She comforted herself by eating a warm, gooey booger.

I still didn't remember this a few years later when the teenage preacher's boy rubbed against me while playing hide 'n' seek. He trapped me on the bunk bed and lay on top of me in the dark. I quit playing hide 'n' seek with him.

I didn't remember Grandpa Chester when playing doctor with Bobbie. I didn't remember this when I straddled the porch fence, rubbing on the edge. It felt good at first, but then I realized the sharp edge had made me bleed into my panties.

That scared me, and I remembered all the preachin' and anxious/angry/awkward instructions from mom about not sinning, and saving your "bottom" for marriage.

I didn't even remember that first molestation the summer vacation in the South, when I was told to sleep in a little bed in Grandpa Chester's room. Later I remembered being half asleep and his standing over me in the dark, touching me. I would never remember the details.

2. Southern Baptists & Rednecks (Or: 3/4 A Virgin)

We moved in my second decade to the DEEP South: back to the land of my mother, father and their peeps; going back quite a few generations. Back to the red clay dirt. Uncle Bob and Aunt Betty also moved back.

It was fascinating. Everything changed. I started my period. Mom had JUST warned me and gave me some information the summer of the move. Pads were provided (tampons never) and I remembered back to mom's church friend whispering:

"Do you have any K-O-T-E-X?"

I knew she was referring to the box in the bathroom, but didn't understand the significance. Mom would wash out my bloody panties and I took advantage of this until I grew older and ashamed of using mom in that way.

Mom did all the things a housewife should do. She waited on us hand and foot. Three big meals per day were made with love, which began to feel like a type of imposition to me. As soon as we sat down to one meal, mom would be talking about the next. My only job was to wash the mountain of dishes.

It got to the point that I couldn't tolerate breakfast. It was always:

"Hurry! Hurry! Eat! You're going to miss the bus!"

It became another competition with Saint, seeing who could eat the most birthday tacos. If I ate 9, he would eat 10. One Thanksgiving after being urged to have more food, dad said to mom:

"If I have one more bite, I'm going to throw up."

"No, you won't."

"Give me your hand."

She held out her hand and he promptly threw up in it. That was in front of about a dozen assorted family members, mostly from mom's side. He thought it was funny, mom was mortified.

A little black and white tv appeared in the living room. Little brother Nate watched cartoons, but *I* was technically a woman and found them silly. I loved watching *I Dream of Jeanie (NBC)* and *Bewitched (ABC)* after school.

Mom sewed a couple of frilly pantsuits and a pair of culottes-the only pants I had ever worn, except for snowsuits up north as a toddler. The girls at the new school wore shorts, halter tops and mini skirts.

It was difficult for me to understand a lot of the new southern people. I had to really listen hard and speed up their accent in my mind, as if I was playing a 33 1/3 record on 78 rpm. I determined I would never talk like that. Most of the members of the two brother's families began taking on a southern drawl.

Mom's parents were tobacco farmers and old-timey Democrats, just over the border in a neighboring county/state. Grandpa Roman always wore overalls. Grandma Della liked poetry and believed in education.

She called me, "My little butterfly."

My youngest uncle, Kent, was a few months younger than me, and seemed more like a cousin. Mom and Grandma had been pregnant at the same time. He had dark hair like the three of us. He seemed a little older, being like an only child with all his siblings already grown and living in their own homes.

We climbed the trees, having favorite seats in the old apple tree. One day we had the bright idea to throw little hard green apples at passing cars from up in a taller tree, closer to the country road. A truck stopped and turned around, the man driving had an angry look on his face. We went running and hid in the old can house.

One afternoon, Kent and I shared a sweet, secret and very innocent peck on the lips; up in the apple tree. We would always be close, even without seeing one another for months or years.

Later, Uncle Kent's wife never had more than two words to say to me: 'yes' or 'no' in answer to any questions. She talked with animation to my parents, laughing loudly and often at dad's silly jokes. Maybe she just held my differentness against me. I always wondered if Kent had told her about the kiss. Maybe she was jealous of the double dates we had later in our teens, knowing I had fixed Kent up with a couple of my friends. We had so much fun hot-roddin' in his souped up, red sports car.

It became more clear in later years that Kent's wife had a hateful and vindictive side. She openly disdained Kent and seemed to prefer the company of their effeminate, mama's-boy son who never dated or married; who acted like his mom. It appeared from a distance to be a classic case of triangulation, with Kent being the loser. He suffered from depression for many years, like Grandma Della.

While we played, dad built an inside bathroom for Grandma and Grandpa. A favorite game of Kent's, was *Rebels & Yankees*. I had to be the Yankee, having been born up north. Kent and Saint were the Rebels, being born in the DEEP South. They would always win the battles, but I would insist at the end:

"Oh yeah, well who won the *WAR*?"

I remembered playing *Cowboys & Indians* in the North and was very philosophical listening to a future friend in California describe their childhood game of *Illegal Aliens & Border Patrol Agents*.

Dad went to work building our new house. He sawed the boards, wired it, plumbed it, did rock work and everything else except laying brick for the foundation. He would eventually finish painting the sheetrock some years later. He was usually outside at his sawmill and garage, working on 'projects.' He could fix just about any vehicle in those days and was known to even make parts by hand to repair automobiles and houses.

He often described himself as, "Jack of all trades; master of none."

Dad and Uncle Bob had helped with saw milling when they were young, off-bearing the lumber from the logs, as the big saw cut them. Uncle Bob told the sawmill story:

"I was off-bearing the boards as they were cut from the logs. I looked up to grab a board, and saw a bloody leg coming towards me! Grandpa lost his balance and fell into the big saw and it cut off his leg! He buried it in the graveyard where the lake is now. When they moved the graveyard, he had his leg moved to the nearby cemetery with the other dead family members."

We asked, "How did he get around?"

"He made a wooden peg leg for himself."

I was always amazed by the gruesome tale. There were family photos that backed up the wooden leg story. It stuck straight out when great grandpa was sitting. The great grandparents had 12 kids that lived, and Chester was the oldest.

I realized in hindsight that Uncle Bob was like Trump in many ways: bragging, cheating at cards, and he liked to have had a fit if he perceived a slight. He got very angry a couple of times when Bobbie and I beat him and dad at cards.

That *never* happened, and I took the opportunity to rub it in like they did.

"Ha-we beat you! Ha-Ha!"

If looks could kill...He knew better than to say or do anything directly to me, his niece. Instead, he angrily slapped the cards out of Bobbie's hand. Dad laughed along with me and Bobbie. Up until that point, I had just seen Uncle Bob as a fun uncle who would play games with us.

Most of his children also became braggarts and couldn't stand for their cousins to better them. They were afraid of their dad, and for good reason. It was whispered to me how he slapped them across a room when he got riled up a couple of times. He was tall and big and he could look mean. He was the kind of guy who would have a used car lot and run for sheriff.

Aunt Betty made the older girls/daughters do all the chores and take care of the younger kids. I saw her smack Bobbie up the side of the head with a hairbrush one day.

I heard her say many times:

"Just wait till your dad gets home..."

She had periods of dark depression and would go from totally letting herself go, to dressing up for church. She did better the few years that she worked outside of the home in the South. She was always nice to me.

Not one of those cousins got a degree (although one came close). They threw off on educated people until finally some of THEIR kids graduated from college. THEN it was all over Facebook and you would have thought they were the smartest kids in the world. Several more of those kids would go to jail.

Mom and dad closely resembled a southern version of the tv couple, Edith and Archie Bunker from *All in the Family (CBS)* . They even had some physical similarities, but mom had longer hair and dad had a crewcut in those days. Mom/Edith showed her love by taking care of all of us and deferred to dad. Archie/Dad was overtly racist, although not to the degree of his elders.

Archie's dad, Chester, had a black dog named Nig@#*. When the preacher visited, he became Blacky. Although that kind of racism often runs through generation after generation, on account of Sunday school teachin' and all; I believed in Jesus' love, which was without discrimination.

One day while watching *Mod Squad (ABC)* on tv, dad came through the living room and said in a joking manner,

"You must be a nig@#* lover."

I retorted: "Dad, I don't believe Jesus would agree with that attitude!"

I remembered this later when the so-called 'Replacement Theory' had become a shrill racist doctrine on the Far Right.

I wanted to argue, *Who did WE replace? We will ALL be replaced someday.*

Dad mostly kept overt racist comments in check after that, but ALWAYS tried to 'get your goat,' from the preacher on down to the youngest family member. Family and friends usually either really loved him and laughed with him, or barely tolerated him. Mom's family mostly fell in the latter category.

I told dad after one of his covert racist remarks:

"I have prejudices too!"

Dad looked surprised and said, "Oh yeah?" He could not guess what they were.

"Rednecks and Southern Baptists," I heehawed.

Dad laughed with me ruefully, saying, "I guess you got me on both counts."

Actually, I liked *some* rednecks and Southern Baptists. It was the willful ignorance and the judgy fundamentalism that tried to enslave me, that I abhorred. My best friend from high school graduated from Bob Jones University, one of the large evangelical colleges in the South. She married a preacher. I still consider her my friend.

The Southern Baptist Convention was equated to the "State Church of the Ex-Confederacy," in the fascinating book: *American Theocracy* by Kevin Phillips. That was MY experience. There were many smaller sects that were similar to Southern Baptists; but in the South, and the larger country, Southern Baptists were by far the largest denomination that espoused the dogma of the fundamentalists/ evangelicals.

I decided early on that I would NOT be an Edith, to be bossed around and walked on. I threw off on dad about how he treated mom. I had to learn to take the good and leave the bad: not to be overly critical, but not to be a doormat. Many of my future relationships were flushed down the toilet in the process of trying to strike a balance.

GRANDPA CHESTER AND Grandma Fawn lived within shouting distance of the new house. We'd walk over to their house and watch westerns and *Hee Haw* (CBS) on their tv. Grandma told a couple of funny stories about her and grandpa.

"On our wedding night, Chester told me to stick my head under the covers. He held my head trapped, while he farted."

We thought that was hilarious. Another story was about playing board games.

"I beat your grandpa at checkers one day. He got so mad, he picked up the board and let the checkers slide down the board into the fire."

We asked, "What did you do, Grandma?"

She said, "I just laid the board on top of the checkers in the fire." We all laughed.

One day when 10 year old Pam was washing the dishes and mom and grandma were in the garden, Grandpa Chester came up behind her; grabbing her by the crotch, lifting her slightly off the ground. Years later when Trump said, 'I just grab them by the pussy,' and then mom said she was going to vote for him, Pam felt betrayal and rage.

Another day when Pam was on the front porch reclining on a couch reading, Chester came in, trapping her with his body while trying to rub the outside of her panties under her dress.

He said, "Someday when I get you alone up in the woods, I'll do something that feels really good."

Pam learned to stay away and declined to go to the grandparent's house most of the time. That didn't stop Chester. He decided to go to church with his son's family. That was the only time she remembered him going, although grandma went often.

He positioned himself in the backseat between Pam and Saint. It was a cold winter and the heater didn't work very well. He said something about keeping Pam warm, throwing his heavy long overcoat over them. He proceeded to force his hand between her legs under her dress and began rubbing away. Pam was pissed and frozen in fear that someone in the car might find out what a sinner she was. She stiffened her legs and just managed to keep his fingers from going inside her.

Bobbie and I always talked about everything and could practically read each other's minds (like our fathers). It turned out Chester had molested her too. That was maybe the second reason Bobbie became a druggie and a thief.

We young cousins determined to catch him in the act. The next time everybody was at grandma & grandpa's, Bobbie went onto the back porch where he was sitting alone. I listened off of the porch, in the dark, giggling a little. Chester seemed to realize he was busted and that people were talking. He never touched either one of us again and we girls felt powerful and closer than ever.

Later when Chester died of cancer when we were in our teens, we were relieved. We had beaten him. There was never a question of telling the folks: it was understood by us girls that we would be blamed and considered sinners, and that nothing probably would have happened to Chester.

I went into a depression during those days, lasting on and off for years. My eyesight became worse, with awful headaches. I had to get glasses. Later in my 20's I read that it was 'fear of the future' that was the psychological cause of near-sightedness, in Louise Hay's book *Heal Your Body A-Z*. I did eye exercises and believed if my eyes could get worse, they could improve. I went from 20/200 to 20/80 in my worst eye. The other went from 20/80 to 20/20. The eye tests were clinical proof of positive thinking.

After getting a sunburn one summer, I began peeling off the dead skin. I also had a lot of mosquito bites. From that time I struggled with picking at my skin. Unfortunately, it was my face and the cuticles around my fingernails that suffered the most. I tried my best to cover the sores with make-up. I also chewed on the inside of my lips.

At times of great stress I didn't seem to be able to stop. It was an unconscious thing. It took me several years to get it under control, and it would come back to plague me during trying times. It made a lot of sense later as a mental health professional when I saw that there was finally a diagnosis for it: Body Focused Repetitive Behaviors(BFRB). I only ever wanted to be "normal"; to right the wrongs, to figure out how be happy.

———◦———

THE ONE BRIGHT SPOT in my life was music. The old upright piano had moved with the family to the South, at mom's strong request. It was in the basement and the keys would stick in the summertime from the dampness. It would dry up in the winter, when the wood stove was fired up.

I only had piano lessons for about a year up north. I wrote: A-B-C-D-E-F-G-A-B-C... on the white keys and circled the sharps and flats in an old hymnal. I began teaching myself, beginning with the easier songs. I knew all the hymns, which made it easier to tell if my playing was accurate. I worked my way through some 500 hymns and the nice new preacher allowed me to be the church pianist. I would wait until he would call me up after the first prayer. I played the piano at church for five years or so.

One of the funniest family stories was a much repeated church scene. Mom and Aunt Betty, with all their kids, went to church one Sunday evening. Dad and Uncle Bob were working together at the prison over the mountain, as guards.

We got there late while the congregation was standing in prayer, eyes closed. At the "Amen," everyone sat down. Young cousin Tory, sitting with Nate in the pew in front of his older cousins turned around with a funny look on his face. He was holding up the preacher's hat with his thumb and pointer finger. He had squished it flat.

Well, that did it. The cousins began to snicker and couldn't stop! We were dying to bust out laughing, our faces red, holding ourselves in a vain attempt to avoid getting in trouble for disrupting the service. It was all in vain, as Bobbie couldn't hold it in. Aunt Betty took her outside and spanked her.

At school I saw the new, young and beautiful band director who was looking for students. I begged mom to join band, and the four young cousins all joined and got trombones. Mom had asked Mr. F if they could be played at church, and he said,

"Of course."

We DID play a few times in church, getting hymnals for Bb (B-flat) instruments. We even played on the local radio once and for a talent show. We called ourselves "The Horns of Jericho."

After the first year; a younger, male drummer and I were given permission to go over to the high school twice per week for band. Mr. F picked us up and then returned us to the elementary school. Another year went by and I was made 'First Chair' trombonist. All the girls had a crush on Mr. F and all the boys admired him.

With all the changes at the new school, in the new town in the DEEP South; and now being a young woman, I had found the group I fit in: band. I played in the pep band at basketball games, but was not allowed to go on overnight band trips.

The music saved me. I began to play a cheap transistor radio I bought with saved allowance and birthday money; all night on low, at my ear. I would often read or listen to music all night long, placing a towel under my door so mom wouldn't know I was still up.

I was placed in the Gifted Program at school and got to miss another regular class each week. I was at the head of the class in those days before I began putting most of my energy into the boys. There were only a handful of students in the Gifted class and we got to do various interesting projects and studies.

I was told my IQ was about 140. Later in life my son and granddaughter would also be in the Gifted Program, although the names of the programs changed. I felt special. I remembered our old preacher calling me, "My little PhD." I surmised that dad was a genius in some ways. He was well read and always had well thought out and original ideas.

I always had little boyfriends that I was 'sweet on' from about 1st grade on, changing frequently. I began to kiss boys and more and more of my attention went there. I would have been good at sports, being the fastest runner in my class in fifth grade. I beat the fastest boy in a race at recess—the boy I had a big crush on for more than a year. I often had scabby knees from running faster than my legs could carry me on the paved playground. However, mom wouldn't allow school sports because it involved indecent uniforms and too many late night trips with boys. Saint, on the other hand, played sports for several years. That was different. He was a <u>boy</u>.

I *WAS* ALLOWED TO GET A summer job at 14, at the local Dairy Barn. Dad knew the owners and trusted them. The 30 something year old son, Johnny, who ran the restaurant flirted with all the girls. He began to take an interest in me and would stay around at closing.

He kissed me a time or two. Once in the back he took my hand and put it down his pants; onto his bare, hard penis. I was shocked. A few days later he kissed me and pulled me into one of the small, dirty bathrooms. He kissed me and began to touch me. Before I knew what was happening, I was on the floor and my pants were being pulled off. I protested, being on my period and feeling embarrassed when the double pad; partially saturated, became visible.

He tried to penetrate me, but I was a virgin and it hurt too much. I was afraid, my body stiffened and I turned my head as tears began to fall.

He stopped with a little smile, saying: "I didn't realize you're still a virgin." I had told him, but he didn't believe me, apparently.

I told my secret to three friends I trusted. I told Bobbie, my little boyfriend and my best friend. They promised to keep my secret, and then they each told one other person. Soon everyone knew. It quickly got back to dad and all over the school.

Dad took me over the mountain to the next town for a physical examination. The doctor reported the hymen was torn, but that I was still "3/4 a virgin." Dad had a long talk with me in his truck about boys and sex, giving me permission to touch myself in private.

He explained, "You cannot commit sin by touching your own body—it's yours."

I thought, *Finally—something that isn't sinful.*

Mom's reaction had been, "You need a spanking. You're grounded until you're 18."

The spanking never happened and 18 became 16. I thought seriously about running away, in the mean time. It seemed highly unreasonable that I would not be able to date like my schoolmates when I had been the victim of an almost statutory rape.

Dad had asked, "Do you want me to take Johnny to court?"

Mortified, I said, "No."

He told the story of Fanny, who apparently hung out at the county dump, propositioning men. He called her a "whore." I knew Fanny and liked her well enough. She was friendly, if a little silly.

I responded, "So if Fanny is a whore, what are all the men that take her up on her offer?"

Dad had to admit, "Well, of course the men are no better than she is." Although Archie was sexist, he always wanted his daughter to have equal rights.

Dad was also in my corner when I got in a fight with the bully of the school. The bully was built like a strong, tall boy and she was always itchin' for a fight. It started with Myrna making fun of a retarded girl at the lunchroom table. 'Retarded' was an acceptable descriptor in those days, changing to 'Developmentally Disabled' when I began my career.

I was sitting across from Myrna and Kim. Kim was not to be

missed. She would talk to anyone and really stood out, being tall and fat and with bushy red hair. She was even sometimes the instigator of dramatic situations. However, that day she was minding her own business and eating her lunch. I must have had a disgusted look on my face when I looked at Myrna, because the ridicule was then shifted to me.

Myrna said, "You didn't like that, did you?"

I replied very clearly and slightly louder, "NO. I didn't. You're no better than she is." All the heads around us turned in our direction and the lunchroom got quieter.

Myrna had heard the gossip about the almost statutory rape and began taunting me in front of everyone. I felt my face get hot. I had never backed down from a fight with my older brother and I didn't back down now.

She said, "Meet me outside at recess."

I said firmly, "I'll be there." I was happy to agree to fight her, anything to get her to shut up and quit embarrassing me publicly.

Word got around, as it always did when a fight was brewing. Bobbie walked out with me to where a small crowd had gathered. As I walked up to Myrna, I turned and handed my glasses to Bobbie. Before I knew what happened, Myrna hit me on the side of the face before I turned around and had me on the ground. She was on top of me.

I thought quickly, *If I don't get her off of me, I'm a goner.*

I gave a big heave, and jumped up quickly, grabbing a big handful of her beautiful, long black hair. I yanked her head down, holding the fistful of hair for my life. With my other fist, I began raining blows on the side of her face as fast and hard as I could.

Before I knew what was happening, the boy's coach came and broke us apart. In the principal's office, Myrna had a slight smile.

She said, "I'm sorry for saying, 'you suck dick.'"

I came home filthy from rolling around in the dirt and a bloody nose, thinking *I'm in trouble.* I was surprised that they didn't blame me when they learned some of the details. I never got suspended. They just gave us a talking to in the principal's office.

Dad took me down in the basement and taught me how to fight. He encouraged me to write: "R-O-C-K" on the knuckles of my fist, in response to the bully's whine that I had hit her with a rock; trying to explain away her black eye! Hell, half the school had *witnessed* the fight firsthand.

That got me into trouble with my Math teacher, but I responded defiantly: "Dad told me to do it."

When the little school paper came out next, there was a small photo of me in a collage of the week's happenings/sayings. The caption underneath said, "The Champ." I wondered for years who had done that, probably someone in band—several of them worked on the paper.

To Saint's credit, he also got in a fight with one of the male bullies, Myrna's brother. He was defending and protecting his little sister again. He never told me the details, and I didn't witness it.

Dad fixed up a filthy old car for me shortly after that. I had not been impressed when I first saw it. He cleaned it and tuned it up, and displayed it the second time with a flourish and a grin.

He said, "How do you like them apples?"

It was beautiful: baby blue with a black top. It was a huge boat of a car. I payed him $200 a year later when I was allowed to get another job. I always paid for my own gas and oil, and even paid a bit of the insurance, which was on dad's plan. I had learned to drive in mom's 4-speed Opel, driving up and down the dirt road at 14. Saint also had an old, sporty car that dad fixed up.

Dad drove like a maniac on the mountain roads. On a trip to the eye doctor I had laughed at sliding on the bench seat in back, from one side to the other as we went around curves. Seatbelts were not required in those days. I always thought about dad years later when *I* was the one driving like a maniac, up and down the mountain.

I drove to school the last two years and began 'courtin.' I continued to spend more and more energy on boys and to meet them at school and church, finding ways to hide and touch and grope with them. I never went "all the way" with them, being afraid of getting pregnant and going to hell.

The Driver's Ed teacher at school tried to feel me up one day when I came into the empty classroom to pick up my forgotten coat. He was known around the school as being 'handsy.' A popular Math teacher was reportedly fired some years later for having an inappropriate relationship with one of his students.

Yet another one of my teachers, in that very small school, (my senior class size was 52); got in trouble with the law. He was a very religious man, who would one day beat up his wife, leaving her in very bad shape. He had reportedly gone to jail or prison for a while and could never teach in that town again. He was Saint's favorite teacher.

Saint got angry at me decades later, because my opinion of the abusive felon had changed. He wagged his finger at me at mom's birthday dinner party, saying,

"You're not perfect. You've done things..."

I said, "I'm not going to argue with you."

3. Lyin' Liars
(Or: Born Again AND Again...)

Senior year was a bust. I had been counting down the months with each menstrual period since I was 14. *48, 47, 46...3, 2, 1* and I was finally a legal adult. I understood my real life would not begin fully until I had full control of my life.

The Archie and Bob families grew further apart as the cousins all grew up and began running off to get married young. Saint went to college for a year and determined it wasn't for him. They all found jobs or got married and began moving away.

I found out that the would-be statutory rapist had gotten several teen girls pregnant. I had felt like my life was over at 14. Our beloved band director, Mr. F, got married and moved all the way to Alaska, precipitating my dropping out of band.

Although I was finally allowed to date at 16, the pickings were slim in the rural south. However, my hormones were raging. I went to four proms and felt guilty for years because I had not only danced, but had LOVED dancing. I had promised not to. Later when the movie *Footloose* with Kevin Bacon came out, I felt better.

Even THE BIBLE said, "...*There's a time to dance.*"

The last prom date was with a boy from church. He was so grown up looking with his full beard and he worked regularly, besides finishing high school. He was good looking, similar to Barry Gibb of the Bee Gees.

I had tried to get away and go to college. I went to a religious college in Nashville that was related to our church, for about a month.

Church boyfriend Nick said, "Will you marry me?"

It was after a make-out session and I thought I was in love. In hindsight, I did not know what love was. After having sex clumsily a time or two when he visited in Nashville and I was beginning to look at the college boys; he gave me an ultimatum: get married, or else.

We noted that there was blood on the sheet after our first time. We were happy and proud: I was still technically a virgin. I worried constantly about going to hell for being a fornicator.

Nick upped the ante by telling me in a scared voice, "The doctor found a black spot in my lung." He led me to believe he would not live long (he has lived past 60 so far).

I dropped out of college; crying the entire way home. I had to pull over at one point because the tears made my vision too blurry. We got hitched a week later, outside at the lake, with only family and our pastor.

Everyone seemed to think I was pregnant, evidently. The preacher asked about the dates later when our son Clay was born over a year later. I had thought many times: *Shoot, my life is over.* Nick wanted a baby and I decided there was nothing else for me to do.

I was not a house-wifely type, having vowed not to be like Mom Edith; so I got a job at the local sewing factory. All day long I sewed the 'seat seam' in dozens of men's pants. At breaks and at lunch the air was thick with smoke from smokers. Nick did not want me to work and I became nauseous and 'give out' with my pregnancy, so I quit.

Nick was smart and funny and good looking, but he was definitely a redneck. He loved his pick up trucks and guns and he came from a very poor family. His sweet mom worked at a factory to raise five kids, while his drunk-ass dad took much more than he ever gave and would then leave for months. He beat on Nick, who bore the brunt of the abuse for the family. His father died some years later; found in a ditch drunk. The family found out that he had a whole other family somewhere, reportedly.

I refused to go around Nick's father (who was meaner'n a striped snake), after he started an arbitrary argument with me while I was pregnant. I had slung the door back on my exit, hitting the chair he was sitting in. He had slammed the door on my pregnant body as I left. I swore he would never see his grandchild. I kept my word, only taking our son to see his paternal grandma.

I was more depressed than ever, feeling like an elephant and breaking out into hives for weeks. My big round, purple belly tormented me. The trailer we lived in had no air conditioning and it was sweltering off the mountain in the DEEP South. I craved pecan pie with ice cream, and gained 50 lbs.

The moment Clay was born, I was a little happier and had a reason to live. I enjoyed breast feeding him, remembering with some embarrassment (and pride) that one of the nurse's had said,

"You have perfect nipples and breasts for breast feeding."

Nick worked most of the time and we began to argue often and loudly. The positives of the marriage were Clay, and the legal and biblically condoned sex. We had license to experiment finally, and I became multiply orgasmic after Clay's birth.

However, we had only one thing in common: Clay. I began to study and ruminate about getting a divorce. I began to look at my religion of birth more closely, searching for an off-ramp.

I finally came to the conclusion that I would rather die than be married to Nick for the rest of my life. It wasn't him so much as having nothing in common and feeling alone. We were very different people who wanted very different things. I wanted Clay to have more. We argued constantly and there didn't seem to be any middle ground. The anger was growing, and knowing murder of myself or others was a sin (*"Thou shalt not kill"*), I surmised it would be much better to divorce.

We had stayed with mom and dad, and then his sister shortly after the birth, selling our trailer that we could not afford on Nick's income. I got a restaurant job and then another and slowly began fixing to escape.

If I had been raised in a liberal Christian tradition, I would most likely have never felt such a need, to reorder my entire life view. I understood that a divorce for a fundamentalist/evangelical such as myself would mean either no religion or no life. Fundamentalism was much more about sin and hell, than Jesus and love and forgiveness. It was an excruciating position to be in. I finally began to take ownership of my life and mind.

I BEGAN DATING AGAIN the moment I knew for sure it was all over. In a short time I got my own little apartment and moved out. Although I was tempted, I knew in my heart I would never return. On weekends I made up for lost time while Nick had Clay.

For the first time in my life, I was FREE. Free to make my own choices, free to make my own mistakes. My depression finally lifted and I felt immensely energized. With a passion, I began working hard and in the little bit of free time, playing hard. I made up for lost time by owning my sexuality and life with gusto.

I had many boyfriends, and that first year as a divorcee was reminiscent of the *Looking for Mr. Goodbar* (Paramount Pictures) movie, minus the murder. I also related to a southern version of *Sex and the City* (HBO) in hindsight, comparing it to that time. I never gave up my number when asked how many lovers I'd had or later when asked how many times I'd been married. I'd just laugh and say, "Too many."

I was dating 4 guys at the same time for a while: an artist who painted over me when his "real" girlfriend returned, a radio DJ who had a footlong schlong, longhaired depressed hippy; and finally young Brent who was a college student. As I was super busy as a single, working mom; I had to narrow it down fairly quickly. It was just too complicated. I began serial dating/marriage relationships that would last 1-10 years.

Nick said one day, "I'd like to have full custody of Clay."

I said, "No. I can agree to half time custody."

Nick took off with Clay at the end of that first year of separation, never bringing him back after the weekend, never calling. I became more and more alarmed and went to find him. He had moved and quit his job. I didn't know what to do.

In a panic, I begged his old employer, "Please tell me where he has gone. My son needs me."

I had to wait over a three-day holiday weekend, to get a court order and have the police bring Clay back, once I found him. It had been almost a month, and I was devastated; thinking, *I might never see him again.*

The police brought Clay home and he was happy they had turned on the police car lights for him. He had been toilet trained, but began bed-wetting again for a time.

He told me, "Daddy said I have a new mommy and I can't see you again."

The divorce was granted, I got full custody and $30 per week child support. Nick never showed up at court. After a short few months of missing several weekend visits with no notice, and missing child support payments, Nick faded away. At first it was for some months and then for years at a time. He owed thousands of dollars in back support at the time he resurfaced years later. Clay was the one lovely thing that came from that first marriage.

———◦———

AT 23 I WAS ABLE TO buy a house in a nice family neighborhood through the FHA program. My payments for a three-bedroom house were less than for a two-bedroom apartment. I learned how to clean my own chimney and repair my own copper pipes. I learned how to keep the half acre yard mowed, and even taught myself how to make wine with the grapes on the back fence.

When Clay went to kindergarten at five, I began college again at 25. I put him on the school bus with a few tears and happily went off to college for four years. I took many dance and music classes, but settled on and completed a BS Psychology degree, graduating *cum laude*.

Although mom and dad had not wanted the life for me that I had chosen, they came to my college graduation. It had been one thing when I attended a church college, but quite another when I began to attend a secular university. Grandma Fawn also attended and it was one of the last happy times with her before she had a stroke.

I realized quickly that I was a liberal feminist, and the Women's Studies course had confirmed it. I had voted for Reagan in 1980, thinking I was a conservative because my parents were. After that I became a lifelong Democrat and feminist. It helped me that the liberal politics more closely matched the teachings of Jesus: full of tolerance, forgiveness and love. He was not dogmatic. He was all about taking care of people and sharing.

I received student aid and had student loans. I worked as a waitress at lunchtime on weekdays. Credit cards were maxed and then transferred to others with 0% interest.

President Reagan cut student aid in the middle of one semester and I had to go on AFDC (Aid to Families with Dependent Children) for the remainder of that semester. I was really embarrassed, but quickly realized that I was doing the right thing. I was a tax payer and that money was there for people like me, when they needed it.

I became a volunteer for battered women, carrying a beeper for a women's shelter a few days per month. I was usually called out in the middle of the night to the police station. I became an advocate for the powerless.

Cousin Bobbie had divorced her first husband after he beat her up several times. I invited her and her daughter to come live with me and Clay and start over. Instead, she went on to date a small time drug dealer who went to jail. Bobbie began doing more drugs and eventually went away for a few months after being caught doing drugs with her underage daughter.

Grandma Della was a believer in education; Edith and Archie, not so much. However, mom DID get her GED in her 40s and I was very proud of her. I even bought her a graduation gift, maybe the only one she got.

Later, I would think about this aversion to education when the Trumpies were in power. Some "friend" on Facebook would post something like: 'Better to have common sense than book learning.' I wanted to reply that maybe it was better to have BOTH, so many have NEITHER. One does not preclude the other. I decided I would rather be ostracized for being educated; knowing a thing or two, rather than be ignorant. I knew my mind was given to me to <u>use</u>.

After the divorce, mom said, "Don't EVER bring another boyfriend or husband home."

I didn't go home for 2 years, although I wrote snail mail letters each month to answer mom's letters. During this time Saint had married a 16 year old and had a son, Aaron. He and Clay would grow up to be close.

Saint's reaction to my divorce was to remind me of a Bible story about '*The woman at the well*':

"Do you remember they used to stone adulterers in THE BIBLE? I think that might be a good idea today."

I asked, "What did Jesus say to the men that wanted to stone the adulteress?"

Saint was silent.

I answered my own question, "Let he who is without sin, cast the first stone."

He seemed to be saying that maybe I should be stoned, since I was dating again and having sex after divorce. However, that did not stop HIM from dating again after HIS divorce a year or so later. It was DIFFERENT for him. His wife had left him.

I told mom: "If I have to act like Saint to be a Christian, I'd rather go to hell."

She was aghast; but Pam, The Sinner, didn't give a hoot. Because

Saint was the "injured party" he was allowed to bring his next girlfriend/wife home. Mom coddled Saint and his now two kids, cooking for and babysitting them several times per week.

In contrast, she had told me: "Don't expect me to babysit for you."

Saint was a 'preacher' for a few years, feeling like he was "called" by God. He preached in a tiny country church for a few years, but after his second divorce he quit. He said something to the effect that he didn't feel like he was a good example. He did go on to have a ministry at the local jail, to his credit.

There were MANY hypocrisies before and after that and I knew I was on my own. I knew I could only depend on myself, in the end.

I vowed out loud: "*I* will be my best friend(BF) and will take good care of myself AND my son and that will have to be enough."

I thought to myself, *In ME I trust. My family will not define me.*

———— ◆ ————

I HAD AN EARLY NEAR-death experience at that time. I was driving home from my waitress job when a teenager forced me off the road. I could only hit the teenager's car or go into a spin. I went into a spin and my car went up and over on its side. I could see a creek or river at the bottom of the cliff I was hanging over.

My life did not flash before my eyes, but I DID feel the presence of a being, perhaps DEATH, in the passenger seat beside me. I thought to myself:

I may die. If I'm alive at the bottom, I better get out of the car quickly. The gas tank is on this side.

At the moment when the momentum of the spin should have taken me off the cliff, I relaxed. I thought, *this will be interesting.*

I was curious what would happen at my death. At the moment I let go, the car miraculously sat back down on its four wheels. From that time on, I was not afraid to die. I had faced death with grace and curiosity and acceptance. I had felt a Divine Intervention. My interest in death and dying issues would increase over the years, leading to hospice work and much meditation on death as a Buddhist. I wanted to know the meaning of life.

————◆————

I MET A BEAUTIFUL, tall musician with long, curly, dark hair in the little southern mountain college town. He loved Frank Zappa, and looked quite a bit like him. We dated for a year. I still had Clay's dad's last name. Paul was a liberal, a recovering Catholic, with some history also of sexual abuse in his family. This would turn out to be the longest relationship I would ever have. We were together a decade and learned a lot. The loveliest thing in that second marriage was the beautiful, daily, music practice sessions. He was a decent stepfather—bonus.

He surprised me at one of his band's gigs. He had set up a table for me up front. At one point, he came over, took my hand and led me up to the stage. He got down on one knee, and asked, "Will you marry me?"

The band played a song for us, and we had a little dance. My BF Sam poured a glass of champagne for us. We were all smiles in the pictures and I felt like I had won the lottery.

He played with his band at our outdoor wedding reception while I danced for him with our friends. We had a yummy Greek buffet and one of my restaurant friends tended the open bar. I had been very nervous, marrying again after divorce and being single for seven years. I had a shot or two of tequila with one of our friends before the ceremony. THIS time, we both hyphenated our names.

Because I had given up music except for pleasure, I felt inspired to be with a musician. He was very talented and sometimes even made a modest living from it. Other times he worked at restaurants or did odd jobs.

I was very proud of him when he recorded a beautiful tape of his original piano music. His new band recorded an amazingly creative

World Beat Jazz album, as well.

He influenced me by sharing yoga, nutrition and 'pagan' religious experiences. We attended a couple of Wiccan meetings/gatherings, nude hippy parties and a couple of native-style sweat lodges. We experienced psychedelics together and learned Tarot and numerology. I also learned to throw I Ching coins; and studied eastern religions and philosophy.

Paul got a gig at the local Unitarian Church, playing his electric bass with their band. I attended with him and even considered briefly, becoming a Unitarian.

When I told mom, she said, "They don't believe in much, do they?" That cemented my decision. I would never be conservative enough or Christian enough for Edith and Archie. Plus, I yearned for a better roadmap, not a wide-open philosophy without much focus, as far as I could tell. It felt to me that they believed in *everything (not that there's anything wrong with that)*.

I joined an Edgar Cayce study/dream group. Cayce was a Christian psychic who had the gift of healing. I put a lot of thought into reincarnation, which Cayce reluctantly accepted as truth. Reincarnation was the only philosophy that could explain certain situations. I became a true believer and it added so much depth and meaning to my long life.

I studied *No Boundary* (by Ken Wilber) in college and became convinced that Buddhism was worth looking into. I decided that being a Wiccan or a shaman was not my path for this lifetime, although I felt they were worthy paths for others. I became very introspective and earnest about changing my focus inward rather than outward.

I took a couple of courses on Reiki from a practitioner. Most of the Christians called this type of healing, 'Healing Touch.' Nurses that I worked with later would sometimes incorporate Healing Touch with patients' permission.

I received the 'empowerments' from the Reiki practitioner, and they were a foreshadowing of the many Buddhist empowerments I would later embrace as a Vajrayana Buddhist. Not surprisingly, Reiki evolved among Buddhists in Asia, although it is a stand alone practice and (especially in the western countries) is usually not associated with religion.

I enjoyed the Don Juan shaman books (by Carlos Castaneda), and that furthered my sincere and enthusiastic interest in death and dying topics. I began to think of Death as my friend, as a mirror to hold up and reflect on; to bring perspective to life's situations.

I tried to remember a quote that saved me a couple of times; a warning from one of my favorite philosophers:

"Beware that, when fighting monsters, you yourself do not become a monster...for when you gaze long into the abyss, the abyss gazes also into you (Friedrich Nietzsche)."

I began my career working in a group home for severely emotionally disturbed (SED) adolescents. I was taught physical restraint techniques which were put to use weekly. The population of classified Willie Ms was often physically aggressive. The workplace felt like a war zone must feel like at times. I became hyper alert and learned much about basic human nature.

———————◉———————

AFTER TWO YEARS, PAUL and I craved a change. We were tired of living in the DEEP South where we had to struggle emotionally, being very different in our thinking to most of the folks we knew. Clay did not like his school and was also ready for a change.

Younger brother Nate lived in Southern California. He had moved there when he was in the Navy. He had gotten a college degree, mostly paid for, due to being a veteran. He helped the little family of three move, giving a friendly place to land and begin.

Mom and dad came for a visit. They had relented when I remarried after being divorced for 7 years. Mom and Saint had even come to the wedding. Dad's excuse was his 20th high school reunion, which had been the same weekend.

We had a lovely time, going to see the sights. Dad lugged around his bigass movie camera. One afternoon after lunch, we were sitting around the living room chatting. The conversation turned to dad's sister who had left home as a teenager, to marry. She had charged a bunch of baby clothes to her dad Chester's account before she left. It was the gossip that he was having an affair while his wife was pregnant.

Dad said, "I don't know why she did that. I'm not aware of anything he ever did to her."

I said, "Do you think he might have molested her?"

Dad stared at me in disbelief, "Why would you say such a thing?"

I glanced at Nate: he knew about the molestation. Nate and I talked about everything, and especially the dysfunctional family dynamics. I could feel my face flushing as I decided to finally tell our parents what Grandpa Chester had done to me all those years ago.

I said, "Because he molested ME...And Bobbie."

They were flabbergasted. A long pregnant silence filled the room.

Mom wailed, "Why didn't you tell us?"

I replied, "Because I didn't think you would believe me. I thought you would blame me and call me a SINNER."

Dad sat there with his head down. I finally asked him, "Do you believe me?"

He said after a moment, "Yeah. I wouldn't have believed Bobbie, but I believe you."

I assured him that I knew for a fact Chester had molested Bobbie too. Dad was crestfallen but clearly not up to discussing it anymore.

He said defensively, "Well what do you want me to do about it NOW? Piss on his grave?"

I understood his limitations. I had been working it all out in my mind over the years; with the help of a bit of counseling while I was going to college.

I said, "No, it's enough that you believe me."

After that conversation, things changed for the better. They gave me a bit of a pass, better understanding some of the choices I had made.

In contrast, when the topic of 'Chester the Molester' came up when Saint was around, he said,

"I don't want to talk about it."

He lives today, in Chester's old house. It gives me a bad vibe still, to walk into that house. And when Cousin Deena ranted on FB about how much she loved her grandparents and how much she loved visiting them, and how other grandkids should want to visit their grandparents, I reminded her:

"The whole family knows that some of us were molested by him in that house—there might be a good reason why some grandkids might not want to visit their grandparents."

Mom remembered a time when Chester had tried to kiss her teenage sister, after she was first married to dad and living with dad's parents. Although mom and dad would never approve of divorce or feminists or Buddhists; their love became more unconditional, more like Jesus' Love.

———●———

WHILE PAUL FOCUSED on his music and finding a new band, I began working at a drug rehab for teenagers out in the mountains. It was a therapeutic community (TC), run like a bootcamp. The residents lived and worked there. Encounter groups were often vicious, but honest. I continued to hone my craft and often supervised shifts. I realized I was good at organization and multitasking. I increased my empathy and had good boundaries.

I saw an advertisement in a "New Age" paper, offering past life regression. I had heard of this and had learned in my Psychology classes that hypnosis could be valuable in uncovering and integrating parts of oneself. I understood that past lives were not nearly as important as this present human life, in which I could make changes and improve. However, I had some questions. I wanted to know who Paul was to me from past lives, since the animosity we felt for one another at times seemed way out of proportion to the happenings of this one life.

I went to the hypnotist and gave permission to be taped, wanting to have a recording of the session. I was willing and allowed myself to become hypnotized. It felt like I was remembering things suddenly, much as when I remembered being molested as a preschooler.

Most of my past lives seemed rather mundane, if somewhat tragic: dying of hunger in perhaps Ireland; living with husband and child in an animal skin shelter, perhaps a teepee; being serenaded in a boat, perhaps in the Mediterranean...but nothing seemed to explain the animosity.

One last attempt was made and I saw a pair of intense, beautiful blue eyes. They were the eyes of my husband Paul in this life. My physical body became warm and then very hot. It might have been a precursor to a severe hot flash period, but this was pure emotion!

You see, he was not my husband in that lifetime. He was my father. He was molesting me. It instantly made complete sense to me. We had both been molested in this lifetime. It explained the weird feeling I had sometimes. It explained the time he teased me about having sex with both him and his old friend from high school, when we had visited up north.

———◉———

AROUND THAT TIME, CLAY spent a very rare summer with his dad back in the DEEP South. He had adjusted well and made friends in SoCal. However, when he returned from his dad's, he had an attitude. His dad had filled his head with thoughts of doing things differently; thoughts of disrespect towards women. When there was a disagreement or when I had to discipline him, he'd say:

"I'll just go live with my dad."

He went back to school and became rebellious. He skipped school a couple of times and was drinking and smoking weed with other delinquents. One day he didn't come home and I finally started calling hospitals and brother Nate.

Paul, Nate and I had a heart to heart. I determined with their support that I would not allow Clay to go off the rails like so many of the kids I worked with.

I had always told Clay, "If you want to, you can go live with your dad when you're 14 or 15." I thought now that *it might be better if Clay had a change of scenery and got out of SoCal.*

I finally heard him outside, acting out in the parking lot of the apartment building. I called him inside.

I reminded him of that option, asking:

"Do you really want to go live with your dad? Is that what you want?"

He said, "Yes."

I told him, "Go pack your shit."

Nate drove me and Clay on his holiday break from college, almost 2000 miles across country while I cried. We arrived at our parents' house in the middle of the night with newly fallen snow on the ground. We snuck in quietly and went to bed. Mom knew we were there when she saw footsteps in the snow the next morning, and began laughing. It was lovely to feel so supported by my family.

Clay's dad could not be reached by phone. Nick's brother got in touch with him and he met me and Clay at mom and dad's house. The three of us sat at the dining table, and Clay became less excited as Nick began to lay out the rules. A summer visit had been one thing, but having a third child to contend with was quite another.

Clay agreed to the rules and Nick agreed to do the right thing, and took his oldest son in. He began parenting almost 14 year old Clay, along with his younger half brother and sister. I felt numb and had run out of things to say.

In a wretched emotional state, I got in a rare shouting match with Nate on the long drive home. We were in rare form, taking out our dysfunctional family emotions on each other. We were both the 'black sheep of the family,' neither one being a Christian anymore. We were very relieved and depleted when we returned home to SoCal.

Not long after the return, mom called and informed us that dad had a bone disease; similar to osteoporosis, with two benign growths in his back. They were close to his spine and that bothered his nerves, causing numbness in his feet. He had to quit his job because he couldn't be on his feet more than three to four hours per day. He filed for Disability at 59. After that, dad would often say:

"I feel so unnecessary."

Paul and I moved to an art deco apartment at our favorite beach after Clay left. We loved the beautiful pier and sandstone cliffs, a block and a half away. It was a small surfer/hippy town. One most inspirational moment at the beach was when the full moon rose behind us, while the sun was setting into the ocean.

———— ◉ ————

ONE DAY AS I WAS COMING home from work at the rehab, I heard a haunting, surprisingly familiar, chanting sound coming from the apartment across the hallway. Toni explained she was a Buddhist, when I asked her about it. She promptly invited me to a Buddhist meeting and spent time explaining the tradition.

Toni said, "I am a member of the Soka Gakkai—a large Japanese, Buddhist lay organization, of the Mahayana branch."

It was headed by President Daisaku Ikeda (3rd president) for decades with 12 million followers at that time, including about 10% of all Japanese. They had 1000 spiritual centers in 192 countries, worldwide. I would soon visit one of the largest abroad.

They emphasized *Kosen Rufu* (world peace). They fostered peace, education and culture. In the US there was a sizable membership of blacks and asians; and in California, hispanics. I felt that it really encompassed a cross section of the population and was inclusive. That was a huge difference from the white bread services I attended during my childhood. Some of the famous practitioners of the time were Herbie Hancock, Tina Turner and Patrick Duffy.

Toni continued, "It was founded by Nichiren Daishonin, born in 1222. He was considered a bodhisattva. He taught that the Lotus Sutra contained the highest teaching, suitable for the 3rd age of Buddhism. They advocated chanting of its title/Daimoku as the path to Buddhhahood."

She chanted, "Nam(u) Myoho Renge Kyo, Nam Myoho Renge Kyo, Nam Myoho Renge Kyo..."

The longer liturgy booklet had portions of the *Expedient Means* chapter and *The Life Span of the Thus Come One* chapter from the Lotus Sutra. It was recommended to chant the entire liturgy (Gongyo) twice per day and then the title/Daimoku as many times as possible.

One was to sit in front of the *Gohonzon*, the object of worship at the time. It was a scroll with the words of the Lotus Sutra, signed by the masters of the tradition. It was like a mirror into the condition of the mind and soul and allowed one to focus and concentrate.

I knew beyond a shadow of a doubt that I was already a Buddhist. It was like a flash of lightening; a moment of recognizing karma, an "Ah ha!" moment. It must have come from a past lifetime. I unreservedly converted to Buddhism, formally and wholeheartedly, at age 34. It was meant to be. Everything had been leading up to that moment.

I had given up finding religion until that point. It had been about 15 years since I'd unreservedly been a member of my parents' religion. I had enjoyed reading eastern philosophy, and dabbled from time to time.

Brother Nate and his long time Taiwanese girlfriend attended the Gohonzon deferral ceremony, as did Paul. They had no interest in going to Buddhist teachings with me, but at least they supported my conversion. I was very joyful and continued to practice in the Soka Gakkai tradition for the next 13 years, learning and growing in my new faith.

In the new fervor over my newly chosen religion, I had a dream about Jesus. In the dream, I was looking into another room and saw an attractive young man with long dark hair. I started walking towards him, and realized:

"It's Jesus!"

I quickly began trying to explain to him: "I didn't become a Buddhist because of YOU..."

I looked into his loving eyes and KNEW. He knew everything about me and he loved me. He held no judgement against me. I fell to the ground and prostrated myself at his feet. I knew he was an Enlightened Being.

I woke up. I was happy. I didn't know any Christians personally who had dreamed about Jesus; almost like a vision. I would always feel the love of Jesus, Buddhist or not. I had not turned my back on Jesus, but on the hypocrisy and hatefulness of the evangelical/fundamentalism.

A Jehovah's Witness, walking down the sidewalk, would interrupt me as I was loading my car outside one day. The older lady asked,

"Are you 'born again?'"

I thought for a moment and replied, "Yes, Ma'am. I'm born again...And again and again. I'm a Buddhist."

The conversion would be part of the reason I would choose to go to Asia: land of the buddhas. A deception by another husband would clinch the timing. I would recognize a karmic pattern soon: fall in love easily, get married quickly, uncover a big lie and divorce. I realized: *I must've been a Big Phat Liar in a past life.*

I WAS HAVING AN EARLY midlife crisis, becoming plumb worn out. My only child, the beautiful boy Clay, had moved across the country. That provoked a period of grief and lessened my tolerance for what was not working.

Before our wedding, I had asked Paul, "Have you ever had sex with a man?"

He said, "No."

I asked, not because I would have definitely left him, but because he had some effeminate ways and looked and acted androgynously. I also looked and acted androgynously at times, having super short spiked hair like some of my favorite female musicians: Joan Jett and Pat Benatar. I probably would have been a tomboy if mom had allowed it.

Paul's Big Lie came out: turns out he enjoyed having sex with men. His male, ex-lover friend had attended our wedding at his invitation. The problem was the lie.

He said, "I was afraid you wouldn't want to be with me if you knew."

Although our sex life had been adequate, it was not the playful and intense passion that I had become accustomed to in my wild years. Paul always wanted to take me from behind while lying on our sides.

I had considered a homosexual tryst a time or two. I had been approached by women a few times while dancing in clubs. I had been tempted, but was attracted primarily to men. I liked men. I didn't know what to do with a woman. I had more boyfriends than one would ever need in a lifetime, so had not felt the need to experiment.

———◦———

CLAY STAYED IN THE DEEP South with his dad. Paul and I moved back for a brief time, to be sure Clay was okay. He was. He was so busy with school, working with his dad and beginning to date, that we only saw him a couple of times.

I got a job during that interlude, at an abortion clinic as a counselor.

That was one unique experience, especially in the DEEP South, where abortion is a SIN. It didn't matter what the circumstances were: incest, rape, the life of the mother; or the health of the embryo.

There were protestors every week with graphic signs, yelling at the desperate women who drove in. Paul and BF of the last decade, Sam, had been recruited by me as volunteer escorts for the scared women. A couple of times the clinic was shut down unexpectedly, due to bomb threats.

I did a lot of soul searching and believed wholeheartedly that women have the right to make decisions about their own bodies. Period. I decided if I truly believed that, I should be willing to put myself on the line. By the same token, I thought if someone believed in war or in death penalties, they should likewise put their lives on the line. They should be willing to pull the trigger, to turn on the juice to the electric chair and watch them die.

What was NOT cool, was to call oneself "Pro-life" and then advocate for war and death penalties with no belief in any kind of simple gun control that could save so many innocent lives. Besides, most of the pro-lifers in practice were pro-*birth*, being very unwilling to help young mothers and their children in need. They voted mostly AGAINST social programs, afraid a few of their tax dollars might be wasted, and/or go to minorities.

I never had an abortion myself. I didn't like the IDEA of abortion. I had a dream about my own birth: I'm looking at my beautiful young (18 years old) mother, she is holding a beautiful newborn baby girl, looking down at her with eyes full of love. In the next moment, *I am* the baby, looking up into my mother's eyes.

Different religions have different ideas about when the spirit/soul goes into the body of a baby. Some think it is at the moment of conception. Some think at the 'quickening,' when the fetus moves or when the heart begins beating. Some think just before birth. In my dream, it was after the birth. Only gods or buddhas know for sure.

THE ADVENTURES OF A SOUTHERN BUDDHIST

We always gave the women a 6 month supply of any kind of birth control pills they wanted, that was on hand. Most of the women were Christians and they struggled. Not infrequently, they were sent home without the abortion. It would not be performed if they were not sure or if they were too emotional. Some of those same women that had abortions would later become protestors. They wanted the choice for themselves, but not for others.

It was so interesting and distasteful that people would fight for THEIR freedom to do whatever they wanted, but would then try to force everyone around them to live their lives as they did. They would call the truth a lie, would make lies out to be truth; all to control and force their beliefs on others.

My job was to explain the procedure, give out the pain medication and to listen to the women's trepidations and advocate for their wishes. Judgement was not a part of the equation. A Christian or an atheist, a teenager or a premenopausal woman were all treated with respect. I held their hand if they wanted, and witnessed the abortion; handing the doctor items, as requested. I took them to the recovery room and talked with them about birth control. Most of them never came back, didn't need to. However, there were a handful that returned a time or two, using abortion as a type of birth control.

I never regretted my service to those women. I did it for the right reasons and the majority of people in the USA believe in a woman's right to make decisions about her own body to this day, regardless of what the new Trumpie Supreme Court would do in the future.

One of my favorite books in college was *The Handmaid's Tale* (by Margaret Atwood). It has since become a tv series with several seasons. It is gruesome and it is dark. It is what can happen to women when fundamentalist dogma takes hold and religion is twisted. It is a cautionary, dystopian tale worth heeding.

4. A Year in S. Korea, The Land of the Morning Calm

It was clear that Clay intended to stay with his dad. He had been told he would be there at least a year. He would not be allowed to play his parents against each other from the far reaches of the country.

Paul and I began fixing up an old yellow school bus as a camper, to return back to SoCal. It just happened that it was the bus Uncle Kent had ridden in as a child. We went back in our now magenta bus, with a white top.

We lived on the bus in the middle of the city in a hidden spot behind Paul's new band's studio. We took baths under the stars and at the nearby YMCA where we worked out.

Ironically, I worked on Normal Street with emotionally disturbed (ED) children at an alternative school, as a counselor. My skills with physical restraint came in handy again. It was an interesting life, but our marriage was clearly strained to breaking.

It wasn't long until I found a naked picture of Paul, with his erect penis in the forefront. All those old feelings came back, and I knew I had to go. I had talked about going to Asia to teach English and he had thought it was a great idea until I got my passport, applied and was gone 2 months later.

I applied for Japan, Taiwan and South Korea. S. Korea came through first and I thought it was a good sign that their flag is an I Ching symbol, with a yin/yang symbol in the center.

Mom said dad was doing fine, he had just lost some weight. I said I would come back if needed; dad said, 'go.'

I had arrived at the same awful, pivotal point in a marriage, that was turning toxic. I needed a drastic change, be it death or be it divorce and

Asia. I knew that I could forgive if I left; resentments being deadly.

Well, my world literally turned upside down: on the other side of good ole Planet Earth. The next two to three years were easily the most difficult AND the most interesting. Lordy, the entire spatial world had changed, becoming more circular and quite foreign.

I arrived by Korean Air in Kimpo airport in Seoul at age 36. The Kims, the owners of a private *hogwan* (language institute) were waiting with a sign. I found out later that Kim was such a common name in S. Korea that the taboo of a Kim marrying a Kim had finally been broken. They were both Kims before marrying and seemed a bit ashamed of that. Everyone went by their "last" name, their family name. I could never adjust to that in my mind.

There were ~45 million in S.Korea in those days and almost a quarter lived in or near Seoul. There were ~37,000 US soldiers in S. Korea and roughly the same number of S. Korean students studying in the US.

I had a bad cold, probably from all the stress of leaving Paul to go abroad. I bought cold medication in the Japanese Airport, Narita, on the way. It was $14.50 for Contact, 10 tablets. I lost my voice the 2nd week on the job.

Driving through Seoul with the Kims, I was amazed and amused at the many red neon crosses on buildings. I had come to S. Korea to be closer to more Buddhists, but only a quarter of the population remained Buddhist; another quarter having converted to Christianity. The Koreans were tolerant of religion and didn't see the need to mix it with politics. About half of the country was not very religious and/or practiced the earthbound shaman religion which women resided over.

We drove over one of the 16 bridges around Seoul, over the Han River to the little town of Namyangju-si; to Mr. Kim's parents' home with an old metal gate and a very pretty, old tile roof. His parents: "*ajumma*" (auntie) and "*adjosi*" (uncle) were warm and welcoming. The Kim's two sons, the oldest a bit sullen and entitled and the youngest a bit mischievous, took the new foreign English teacher in stride.

That was the beginning of many a delicious meal on the floor with a low folding table with cushions to sit on. The meals always had individual rice and soup with everyone sharing the other dishes, with matching metal chopsticks and spoons. There was always some kind of fish and some kind of kimchi. Napkins turned out to be what I had always used as toilet paper, in a decorative tin where it rolled out. I never got over the strange feeling of using toilet paper at meals, but knew that was silly. It worked perfectly well and made more sense.

Korea felt to me like the 1950s must have felt like in the US. There was a 'can do' mentality and energy; an excitement of getting and having and being free. There was huge national pride.

When it was noon in S. Korea, it was 10:00 p.m. the previous day, in the DEEP South in the US. I was worn out that first month. No time was wasted getting me started the next day at the *hogwan*. I spent all day into evening: about 8 hours. It had been more, until I finally released myself of the burden of arriving early, sitting around in the office with the Kims, having lunch together...

There was a couple of individual classes during the week: one with a nice middle age woman who owned a hair salon. She talked to me about being unhappy in her marriage and wanting to divorce. Another student was a big (for Korean) middle aged man who took me to nice restaurants for conversational English. It felt more like a date, but I knew how to keep professional boundaries. We had delicious bulgogi and bibimbap. His English was fairly good.

I seemed to be the only foreigner (*Miguk*—white person) in the little town, except for another student from a women's class. That student was a Japanese woman who had married a Korean from the same religious 'Moonie' group: Rev. Moon and the Unification Church.

I also had a class of Christian pastors, male and female. They seemed disappointed that their western English teacher was Buddhist.

They gave me a signed Bible as a parting gift at the end of the year. I promptly regifted it to one of my Korean Christian friends, tearing out the one blank page the pastors had signed.

One of the male pastors told a racist joke about god baking people in an oven:

"The whites were not baked enough, the blacks were burnt, but the Koreans were baked just right." They all laughed.

Mr. Kim made a remark about Princess Diana's death, saying: "She deserved to die for divorcing her husband and having an Egyptian boyfriend."

One of the adult woman pastors said, "Half the population loved Diana and the other half hated her."

Wednesdays were reserved for another *hogwan* in the town of Seongnam, run by the Kim's friends, Mrs. Sung and Mr. Seo. Wednesdays meant a bus ride to outer Seoul and a subway ride to another train on the pink line, Namhansansong station, headed south. Altogether it was three hours roundtrip, but I did not wish to be trapped in the Kim's car and then be expected to go out for a late dinner with *noraebang* (karaoke) and *soju* (potato liquor or rice liquor).

The Korean English teacher was Song and we became good friends. She had spent a few months in Seattle, dating a white boy. She was quite a bit shorter and smaller than me. She had a cute round face with a nice smile; and a good sense of humor. Occasionally we would go out with the owners, eating and getting drunk while belting out tunes, many in English. Dried squid was usually served as snacks, along with Asian party mix. I learned to cook squid on the open flame of my stove. You just put the whole dried squid on top, turning it a few times. It was very chewy, almost like rubber, let's call it squid jerky.

Some of the more unusual dishes were very memorable. One came squirming on the platter: baby octopus, cut up. I looked at Song, who laughed at me and began to instruct:

"Get lettuce leaf, get octopus, put garlic and chili sauce; wrap and chew very good, so octopus not stick to throat—what this?" She tapped the little suction cups on their body with her chopstick.

I said, "Suction cup," and indeed, when I picked up the octopi with my chopsticks, the tentacle wrapped around it. It was rubbery and sinewy, but the garlic and chili sauce masked the flavor.

A wonderful *ajumma* brought a delicacy as a gift to her grandchild's English teacher: a crunchy, spicy Frito like taste in the form of whole fried crickets.

She bowed and said, "T(h)ank you."

I said, "Good, good," as I took a bite or two, "Komapsomnida—thank you," with a little bow.

But the meal that took the cake, due to very different cultural norms, was the dog meat cafe. Now, they raise dogs just as Americans raise pigs for food or Pakistanis raise goats for food. They do NOT eat their damn pets. I had sworn to myself to try whatever was offered to me and be grateful. I watched as the table stew pot was set up and the meat was added to the veggies. Another piece was sliced into strips and grilled. It smelled and tasted gamey, like maybe between a deer and a rabbit?

The Kims laughed as I tried it, and said, "Good, good, Pam is Korean," when I continued to eat and enjoy.

After dinner, I found that one of my boots had disappeared. Everyone had taken off their shoes outside the door.

Mrs. Kim ran out, yelling: "No! No!" She chased down the dog that had been chewing on my boot.

The next day I discovered a fever blister on my lip. I could only surmise it was because of the dog meat (maybe due to some internal angst)? Maybe it was a coincident, but I never ate dog meat again. In fact, during the 1988 Seoul Olympics it had become uncouth to eat dog, in order to appeal to more internationals.

I enjoyed the asian pears, persimmon, oriental melon and the famous Korean ginseng. I got a jar of honey and cut up garlic into it as a home remedy to mix with my ginseng tea for good health.

My classes were not infrequently changed at the last moment. The Kims would call on my phone at the apartment they set me up in.

"*Yoboseyo*" ('hello' on telephone).

The work ethic was intense with six classes a day, five and a half days per week. The Korean children loved to sing songs in English and to play *Bingo*. The *Bingo* categories were little pictures that I would say in English, instead of letters and numbers. I struggled to remember the old grammar rules I had learned at my students' ages.

One of the sounds most difficult for Koreans to distinguish was "r" and "l". Instead of saying: "rice," it came out more like "lice." I drew a little picture of bugs, began scratching my head, and had the Korean English teacher explain they didn't want to ask for little bugs to eat. The little kids loved that, laughing and cutting up, pretending to eat bugs off of each other's heads. Their favorite English song was: "I'm Popeye the Sailor Man" (written by Samuel Lerner), and some of the songs from *The Little Mermaid* (Disney) soundtrack.

I worked at Migum Middle School two afternoons per week, and on Saturday. A young married couple, Joi and Duc, would pick me up in their car. I was encouraged to get a blazer and some clogs to slip into when my shoes were placed like the hundreds of others on the foyer shoe shelves.

You could see your breath in the school. They often left doors open and there was only one gas heater in the middle of the room. About the second or third week, my suede blazer got burnt on the gas heater and was ruined.

On the way home, the windows fogged up so you couldn't see. I pointed from my seat in the back to the 'defrost' button on the dash:

"Push that button."

The young couple was amazed that the window cleared up quickly, and asked,

"How you know that?" They seemed to find it incredulous that I had a car as a teenager and could find a magic button on their Korean car.

In 1985 there was over a million cars in S. Korea. By 1997 there was 12 million. Korea soon joined the ranks of the countries that export over a million vehicles per year. However, I mostly saw Korean make vehicles there. There was some Japanese make, but scant few European or American vehicles. Korea ranked 3rd in the world in death by traffic accidents at one point. Indeed, drivers were aggressive, sometimes driving up on the sidewalks and whizzing by kids with an inch to spare.

In other areas, S. Korea excelled. They grew much of their food in long plastic greenhouses in the winter. I would see them while riding a bus through the countryside.

They had the 8th largest subway system in the world, with 8 lines at that time in Seoul. I loved taking the subway and even the crowded buses. What I hated was all the literal shoving of bodies against each other, crowding onto those buses and trains. I would find myself saying, "*Ish*": pronounced 'eesch', their word for 'shit.' I often used '*shilychamnida*,' 'excuse me,' as I dodged and tried to keep from feeling dissed. It was the same, standing in lines. People would crowd toward the counters, screw the queue!

At one time, S. Korea ranked 13th largest economy; 31st highest per capita; but 59th in world in public health standard. That seemed to explain why the average S. Korean woman was 5'3" and 118 lbs. I was average in height and weight for an American and found it quite difficult to find anything in my size in S. Korea.

I enjoyed the little high-rise apartment with the heated floors, traditional for S. Korea. The little hot water on-demand tank in the bathroom for showers was also new to me. The odd shaped washing machine with Korean instruction buttons worked well. One had to step over a ledge to get into the bath/laundry. The red metal drying stand in the kitchen was handy and standard.

The main aggravation was the traditional squat toilet in the hallway which was shared with another apartment. It was ceramic and flush with the floor. The tank was up on the wall with a tiny window to let in air. You had to bring your own toilet paper. It was usually not provided in S. Korea. I sometimes peed in the drain in the laundry/bath to avoid this annoyance. However, my thighs grew stronger and I thrived. Besides, the apartment came with my salary.

The tv had Chinese, Korean and Japanese channels; and one US channel—run by the US Army. It had a mixture of ABC, CBS and NBC programs. Every night as it was signing off, the US national anthem and then the S.Korean national anthem would be played.

The tall multi-use buildings had apartments with oftentimes a grocery store in the basement, or a restaurant. There was oftentimes a church or maybe even a bowling alley higher up.

I quickly learned to calculate: $1 = ₩870. Each month I became a millionaire, making 1, 200, 000 won. I would meet Song at a western style restaurant in Seoul each month, buy her lunch (Pizza Hut, Hard Rock Cafe, TGIF, Denny's, McDonald's, etc.) and then go to Song's bank. She would send some of my money to brother Nate, to cover my few bills back home.

It was a sweet deal: comfort food with a good friend and help with banking. Song would grab my hand walking down the street. It made me feel strange, but it was sweet.

I told myself, *Don't be homophobic, Silly*.

It was common in S. Korea. Girls held hands with and put their arm around other girls. Boys held hands and put their arm around other boys. It was extremely rare to see couples showing PDA of any kind. Only one kiss was observed during the year. A young couple was hiding behind a column in the subway station.

Once on a subway with an ex-pat friend who worked at Airilang TV station; I grabbed his arm while we talked intently, nothing too risqué. He was considerably older and was white. I looked across the width of the train to a male university student glaring my way. I held his malevolent stare while alerting my friend,

"Karl, look at that college kid giving me the evil eye."

He looked over at the student. When he looked, the student finally looked away. On the way off of the subway, my old competitive nature did not resist the urge to give the student one last glare as I walked past, pausing for a moment.

Song was a true blue friend who always took my side, feeling comfortable with western culture while I struggled with understanding Korean culture. She appreciated my ability to say, "No," to our bosses and hopefully benefitted from it. She had a great rapport with our students at Songnam, which was very helpful.

I got somewhat used to being pointed at, with giggles behind hands and the sound of "Miguk" in my little town. I enjoyed figuring out the buses, money and subway system.

It helped that I learned the Korean alphabet. Song had taught me between classes, giggling at my mistakes. It was relatively easy, being phonetic and having only 23 characters. I could sound out words, so my pronunciation did not suck. I could usually make myself understood.

I made several friends—there were some Canadians in the next little village. I went out with Pat several times: to expat gatherings, to party in Seoul, and once on a hike in the woods to a small Buddhist temple.

We knocked at the gate, and the resident nun came out.

"Annyonghasayo, hello," we said with a short bow.

"Annyonghasayo," she replied, with a deep bow. She quickly made tea and soup for us, very hospitably.

Pointing to myself, I said, "I am Buddhist."

It took some effort to try and make myself understood, pointing to a Buddha statue and then to myself. She smiled, with an eyebrow raised. That was one of my favorite memories of S. Korea.

Another time we went to a local public bath. Men and women had separate facilities. First you showered, then mineral hot-hot pool, then warm pool, cold pool...An *ajumma* scrubbed bodies down. The light was dim and the steam was thick. It felt womblike, a nice contrast to the cold, gray winter afternoon.

There were many stares, but no negativity. Pat was very tall and fat, so she got most of the attention. That was one of the few times I got to enjoy a hot bath in S. Korea. I thought several times after that—*I should have enjoyed the public baths more.*

I managed to go all over the country, utilizing my *Lonely Planet Guide South Korea* (by Robert Story and Geoff Crowther). I visited many Buddhist temples (Naejangsan, Soraksan, Kyongju, etc.), often up in mountains (*san* means mountain). They were painted beautifully with the under eaves being several colors and with paintings on the sides (*Tanchong* style). They had big protective statues of animals like elephants (or mythical creatures) outside and some large buddhas.

A swastika symbol often appeared at or on the temple and on maps where temples were. I was incensed to learn that the Nazis had appropriated the Buddhist swastika sign and desecrated it.

One meal with Song's family was at one of those temples—Kwangju, near Cholla buk-do. We shared the 31 mountain vegetables, a special meal at a beautiful old style restaurant.

I had been made up by Song's sister, like a *gisaeng* (geisha). The make-up began to run and deteriorate throughout the day, much to the horror and amusement of all.

The chorus of, "Beautiful," became "*Igo*(oh my god)."

Song and I went to a provincial park—T'apsa, on Mt. Maisan. That was my favorite Korean Buddhist temple. The temple buildings and altars consisted of thousands of large rocks piled up into forms. It was mind boggling, how they got all those rocks to stay in big stacks, big as large buildings. I never saw anything like it before or since. The nuns and monks of Korea wore gray *hanbok*—the traditional pajama like outfit with a big bow in front.

THE ADVENTURES OF A SOUTHERN BUDDHIST

During the national holiday of Sollal, the Kims and their friends in Songnam, all their three children and two other adults, including Song and I; went on a long van trip around S. Korea. We looked into North Korea at one point, behind a big metal fence with razor wire on top and a guard tower.

I said, "It looks like a prison."

"Yes, yes, veddy bad," said Mrs. Kim.

I sat in the very back with the luggage so I could stretch out more. The Kim's youngest son slept with his head in my lap a couple of hours, and I missed Clay.

We went to the ancient Shilla capitol city of Kyongju. There we saw the National Museum, several royal tombs, Pulguksa Temple and the Sokkuram Grotto. The tombs were in or near royal burial mounds, similar to some Native American burial mounds in the US, but bigger: several stories high.

At the yogwan, it was uncomfortably hot. The floor was scorching and there were so many of us packed into the one room.

I asked Song, "Do you think they'd be offended if I slept in the other room?"

She said, "I'll cover for you."

I took my heavy feather bed into the unheated sitting room and slept peacefully on the couch. There was ice on the windows the next morning.

The *Sollal* holiday also honored the elders in the family. I was invited to join in with the Kims during the *Sebae* ceremony. It is a most important tradition of bowing to the elders; a half prostration with the hands and forehead on the ground. It was fun, but awkward. It was a foreshadowing of a time in the future when I would make many prostrations to buddhas.

They served slightly sweet, round rice cakes in pastel colors, called *Ttok*. The elders gave out little red envelopes with money to those who honored them. The sweet *ajumma* reminded me a little of mom, always being warm and welcoming to her guests.

In hindsight, I really appreciate what the Kims tried to do for me, a strange person in a strange land. They included me in many enjoyable outings throughout the year. That trip had been very special, including many historical places in S. Korea.

I was given a subscription to the oldest english newspaper *The Korea Times*. It had many interesting stories. One of the headlines was: *"Over 500 North Koreans executed in public last year."* I got a taste first hand of the forceful animosity between the two Koreas. Once while on a bus driving towards Seoul, some soldiers got on the bus with assault weapons; looking intently and suspiciously, up close into all the faces. They passed right over me, being a white woman.

A North Korean submarine had washed up on the South Korean side and they were looking for the submariners. I was a little freaked out, NEVER having seen weapons like that and in a tight public space. That episode prepared me for seeing the riot police geared up with shields, lining the sides of the steps going down into the subway near the university.

The students often protested and a couple had died during protests. A poll in *The Korea Times* revealed that half of Yonsei University students were antagonistic to the US. They see the US as occupiers, since we have been there since the Korean (Conflict) War. The students did not live during the time of Japan committing atrocities during their occupation between 1905-1945.

The Japanese soldiers took ~200,000 Korean women to be "Comfort Women." That meant the soldiers took comfort by raping the women who were their prisoners. That remained an issue during my stay. The women protested regularly at the Japanese Embassy. The older Koreans love Americans, remembering how they were liberated and how the USA brought Japan to its knees.

Mom's oldest brother fought during the Korean War. I sent him some postcards from Korea and he wrote back.

He said, "Bring me a Communist's ear on a chain."

He went on, "During the Korean War when we killed someone, sometimes we cut off their ear, dried it and put it on a chain."

S. Korea continues to take a defensive stance towards Japan, criticizing Time's use of "Sea of Japan," rather than "East Sea" or "E. China Sea."

I contemplated the politically correct side some have taken in condemning the bombing of Japan. Sure, bombs are not the answer to the world's problems; they are evil. However, the USA had been bombed by the Japanese FIRST. They had held S. Korea and part of China prisoner for years. The emperor of Japan was thought of as a GOD. It would have taken excessive force to stop them, at the very least.

Revenge can taste sweet, at least for a time. I would embrace revenge with husband #3, who I was getting ready to meet. It allowed me to stay with him for a period.

———————⟡———————

I FELT RICH AND FREE, if sometimes a little lonely. I made another close English-teacher friend, Young. She was hired by the Kim's. She had a European fiancé who also taught English.

I was invited to be in their wedding, to stand in for Andrew's mother who could not attend. I wore the traditional *hanbok*—full length dress with big bow, the crinoline slip underneath and little high heels with slightly pointed-up toes. It was slightly short on me and it was a little tight when I breathed, but I never felt more Korean than on that day.

Their wedding was held at Lotte World at the Korean Cultural Museum. It was quite a production, and one of the highlights of my year in S.Korea. There were at least a dozen foreigners along with all the Korean family and friends present. The traditional wedding was exceptionally beautiful and entertaining.

I lit the candle for Andrew's mom and Young's mom lit her candle. We mothers then bowed to one another, the half prostration, and then to the audience. Live roosters were released to fly around and the bride and groom were carried away in traditional hand carried boxes. There were traditional dancers next.

Young told me,"The Korean photographer asked about you. He thought you were a beautiful 22 year old and wanted to propose."

I wore the traditional hanbok that day, all the way back from Seoul to my little town, on train and bus. I got a lot of positive reactions and maybe: respect. I thought, *maybe I should ALWAYS wear hanbok in S. Korea when traveling!*

It was because of Young's wedding that I met Shane (sounds a lot like his Persian/Indian name). I had hooked up with a coupla' nice ex-pats when it became clear that I would divorce Paul, but fell for a Pakistani I met in the subway station.

He was beautiful with an Indian tika mark tattooed on his forehead. He had gorgeous golden brown eyes and spoke several languages. He was almost fluent in Korean, having worked there several years, going to Korea on a work visa. He was proficient at English, although having a strong accent.

I was meeting Andrew at Yungdongpo subway station to practice for the wedding and was running late. The traffic was horrendous, even more than usual. I took the wrong train the wrong way, having never gone to that station. When I finally arrived at the designated station, Andrew was nowhere to be found. I tried to call and leave a page, but it never went through. That's when I saw him. Our eyes met.

He said, "Hello."

I said, "Hello," and smiled.

After making my call and using the restroom, I waited, walking around a bit and looking for Andrew. He never arrived, he had most likely already come and gone.

We passed again.

He asked, "Where are you from?" I told him.

He said, "I thought you were from Morocco."

I asked, "Are you from India?"

He replied, "No, I'm from Pakistan."

Shane had on dress pants, a white turtleneck and a preppy sweater over that. He was only about three inches taller, with a nice solid muscular build, and had a cute butt with nice definition. He reminded me of some of the characters Benicio del Toro would play in the future: having the same intense eyes, muscular body and beautiful brown skin.

After talking for a while, he invited me to dinner. I was starving, having missed the pre-wedding party. We walked to a nearby Popeye's restaurant. Popeye's fast food was a treat...comfort food. I loved Korean food and almost any food presented to me. I had used chopsticks proficiently since my early 20s. Still, it was always comforting to have one's familiar dishes while residing in a foreign country. We had our first long conversation.

We continued to look into each other's eyes. He told me, "I have 'shame in my eyes' because talking and looking into woman eyes." He was so cute, and I was lonely. He told me, "I am Muslim," but he did not dwell on that.

He asked, "Why you are here without your husband or baby?"

I explained, "I'm getting a divorce and my 'baby' is 16 and now living with his father and doesn't need his mom anymore."

It turns out there was a 10 year difference in our ages. He was only 27. He couldn't believe I was that old with a son practically grown.

Shane felt familiar, although he was a Muslim: perhaps a past life? His level of 'extremism' was comparable to my fundamentalist parents back in the States, giving me a comfortable feeling. Mom had been shocked when I'd explained that to her.

I was surprised to learn there were ~20,000 Muslim guest workers in Korea.

After a long and intimate conversation, Shane suddenly said, "Live with me tonight?"

I was now embarrassed. I was no prude and was far from an innocent virgin, but I got shy and blushed, losing my words. The conversation continued and a couple of hours later, he asked again. This time, I was ready and we left the restaurant.

I tucked my hand through his elbow as we made our way through the crowded Seoul night. He looked strangely at me, and I asked,

"Is this ok?" He responded affirmatively.

He picked out some fruit at a stand. Fruit is traditionally for dessert in Korea and expensive. In fact, most things aren't cheaper in Korea.

We finally got to our room and after freshening up, we were sitting side by side on the bed. We were silent. We looked into each other's eyes, and I reached over for a kiss. His lips were full and sensual and he felt so warm. We kissed a few times. He told me later that it shocked him when I kissed so passionately with my tongue and lips. He said that Pakistani husbands were lucky to get a little peck on the cheek. There was no dating allowed in his country.

He told me, "Take off this," tapping on my shirt.

Being an independent young woman who knew what she wanted, I went for it, just as most young men would have done in a similar situation.

I asked, "Do you want to just get naked?"

We removed all our clothes except he left on his little pair of running shorts. I told him to take them off. He was very hard and sticking straight up, almost 11:00. He was shaved—his pubes and under his arms.

We began touching. It had never taken me long and I had gone without real passion for months. I lay down and pulled him on top.

I said, "Look into my eyes."

He entered me slowly, our eyes like magnets. He geared up quickly while we tongue kissed. He had his first orgasm in a few minutes.

He would instruct: "Clean, clean," after each orgasm. It was a religion thing. After a little talking we began again. He got wilder...faster and with more force. The sheets were soaked.

After several times, I just wanted to relax in the tub. Tubs were scarce in Korea and that was one of about three baths I was ever able to take in S. Korea. Most bathrooms were equipped with a large bucket and a small dipper. You filled up the large bucket and dipped water on yourself with the dipper. You were expected to wear plastic slippers. The floor was usually cement, sometimes tile, with a drain in the floor.

The bath lasted maybe 10 minutes before Shane came in, wondering what I was doing. He explained the concept of Muslim ritual bathing. He insisted my hair be washed each time.

I was dying to stay in the tub, but he wanted me again. I was game. We stayed busy most of the night, "finishing" six times. I fell asleep a couple of times to wake up to his WANT again. Monday morning came way too early and I knew what a long subway and bus ride I had, to get home before classes.

Shane said, "Don't break my heart. And please, don't eat pig."

I said, "My heart has been broken, it will heal. I cannot promise I will not eat pork."

He began to assume quickly we might get married and live anywhere in the world together.

He walked me to the train, giving me his sweater to wear. We had big, stupid smiles on our faces. We watched each other as long as we could. We exchanged phone numbers. I went in to teach my classes with a smile still on my face. The usual antics of the Korean kids didn't faze me in the least today.

I realized I would have to get more birth control pills. I had gone back on the pill after cysts were discovered by my doctor. Doc had suggested the pills might help; and the pain did go away, mostly. I hadn't needed birth control pills with Paul. He had a vasectomy before we met. I had brought a few month's supply, along with several large boxes of tampons with me to S. Korea. The *Lonely Planet Guide* had warned it was difficult to find them. It was true—they were mostly found in Seoul at a large department store at that time.

I went to the doctor for an exam, an English speaking female doctor. She gave me a prescription, and instead of $20 per monthly pack, they were $3 per pack in 1997. The next year in Pakistan they would cost 25 cents per pack. They were roughly the same pills in all 3 countries. The 'Asian' pills were imported from Germany and Ireland. I often pondered on that experience during women's health discussions.

Shane called daily, even calling once at the *hogwan*, which I quickly nixed. I preferred to keep my private life private. We began spending a day or two together each week. He often had to work on Sunday. He worked at a recycling company and made considerably less salary than me, although he worked many more hours.

We wandered around my little town, shopping together for '*hallal*' (Muslim's kosher) food that he could eat. He had a lot of food restrictions; including no pork or seafood, except fish. He loved mutton, which was more often goat than lamb. We went into a pizza restaurant.

Shane said in Korean and English, "No pork!"

The waitress nodded her head and repeated, "No pork."

The pizza looked delicious when it came out and we were hungry. I took a big bite of a slice. I then saw a sliver of something that looked familiar:

"No! Pork!" It was Canadian bacon, underneath the cheese. Shane started to get angry, but we conspired and got up and walked out of the restaurant without paying. We had many a laugh about that later.

He gave me a photo of himself in the Pakistani army uniform. He was a Commando and he looked deadly.

I asked him, "Have you ever killed anyone?"

He said, "Yes, of course."

We went to a couple of movies: *Con Air* (Touchstone Pictures), *Air Force One* (Sony Pictures) and *Face Off* (Paramount). Shane was impressed, having only seen one American movie. The theaters were crowded and folding chairs were placed in the middle aisle. They would've been shut down in the US for creating a fire hazard. The movies were in English with Korean subtitles. I found myself being the only one laughing, at subtle western humor that didn't translate.

Later in Pakistan, Shane flatly refused to take me to the movies. It just wasn't done, apparently. Only women of ill repute went to movies in Pakistan, it would seem.

I met some of Shane's Muslim friends, all male. He had helped most of them get jobs. His fluent Korean came in handy and he was often made supervisor of the foreigners at his workplace. There were many foreigners working in S. Korea, both legal and illegal.

They lived many to a small hut, sleeping on the floor. They cooked big pots of food: *halal* meat and *roti* (traditional Pakistani and Indian flat bread). Everyone sat on the floor on a cloth and (using the right hand only) tore off pieces of roti which was used to scoop up bits of meat and overcooked veggies. Everyone drank out of the same, single water glass. They had a broken down outhouse across the path. The hut was very spartan with no furniture.

We went for a drive out in the countryside, driving on the raised paths between the rice paddies. Shane's friends were amazed when they allowed me to display my driving skills on the old 4-speed car. Women didn't drive in Pakistan.

One time they shared a Madonna music video, thinking they were very risqué. I didn't even really LIKE her music. Rumor had it that the men would utilize the coffee shop girls and/or prostitutes for sex. A couple of them married Asian women, already having a Pakistani wife, neglecting to disclose.

One special day, Shane's Korean friends took us all to Seoul Land, the Disneyland of Korea. We made many beautiful photos there, some of which I would later tear up in a rage in Pakistan, precipitating The Incident.

I OFTEN WENT OUT ALONE, feeling more and more confident and safe in S. Korea. I was very moved by Buddha's Birthday Lotus Lantern Festival in May, sponsored by the Korean Buddhist Chogye Order. There were 100s, no more like 1000s of beautiful lanterns glowing, in a lovely parade. I felt very at home, finally being in a country with lots of valued fellow Buddhists. Most Americans don't realize Shakyamuni Buddha was born more than 500 years before Jesus.

I visited one of the huge and formal Soka Gakkai Buddhist centers in Seoul (KSGI) with a million members, including 30 English speaking foreigners. They chanted the same liturgy in Japanese that I did. It was another moment of solidarity of Buddhists internationally: an American in S. Korea, chanting in Japanese. They gave me several little gifts—you could always count on a little hand towel in S. Korea as a gift. I still have it. It has Korean letters on it. I couldn't find t-shirts with Korean writing, and I looked.

I finished reading *The Lotus Sutra* (translated by Burton Watson), and stayed in touch by mail with my Buddhist friends. The SGI newspaper, *World Tribune,* subscription was forwarded to S. Korea.

When I left the SGI service it was late and I decided to stay at a historical old style *yogwan*—Munhwa Inn. It was winter, freezing and the charcoal heated floor was inviting. However, I dived under the weighty featherbed, as the air inside was very chilly. I could see my breath. It was very cozy under the cover.

The next morning I took in some more sights: Toksuguna Palace, Namdaemun Gate and Market, and Chongmyo Royal Shrine.

I went out with my students on field trips a few times: once to a temple nearby with a picnic lunch of *kimpab*. It was like Japanese sushi. Koreans said the Japanese had learned to make it from them. I went with middle school students to volunteer at a home for developmentally disabled on the outskirts of town. We played basketball with the residents and helped with preparation for dinner.

My favorite teen-age Korean girl, Sea, translated for me.

A couple of middle schoolers brought a surprise for teacher one day. They called it "red flowers." The English names are: Garden Balsam, Touch-me-not, Impatiens; it is mildly poisonous to ingest. It was a frozen concoction they had made from the flowers and leaves that smelled like tomatoes. They put a dab on my six smallest fingers, leaving the pointers and thumbs.

I said, "You forgot," pointing to them.

They said, "No. That kills parent. Tradition."

It was left on all night, and the next morning there was a cool orange stain on my six nails that stayed until they grew out.

That was a common young woman thing in S. Korea, much like henna on the hands and feet would be in Pakistan the next year. At all my classes that month, female Korean students would see my nails, pick up my hand to inspect, and nod approvingly, saying,

"Good, good."

I MADE SHANE A NICE big salad for a meal at my apart (Koreans shortened from apartment).

He asked bluntly, "Is this all?"

I was pissed.

I explained as politely as I could, "I work full time and do not keep house and cook. If you're with me, you'll have to get used to it. I expect any man I'm with to do a fair share of the cooking and cleaning."

He never really accepted that until he'd already lost me.

It was a real chore what he could and couldn't eat. In Korea he ate chicken or fish, but no other meat. I made spaghetti for him, but he went next door and bought chicken instead. He bought halal meat one week, which *he* cooked.

In each other's arms that night he told me he'd been a virgin on our "First Night." He used that term often, not knowing the word for virgin, initially. I found it a bit difficult to believe, he seemed like such a sex machine. However, I had no reason not to. He didn't care when I talked about my ex-husbands but blew his top when I brought up my ex-lovers.

There were many debates about religion. He began to talk about marriage. He felt very guilty for having sex before marriage, reminding me of my own guilt at age 18, regarding sex with Nick.

It became clear to me that in order to stay with Shane, I would have to marry, yet again. He could never go to the USA and I could not go to Pakistan unless we were married or about to get married. It was illegal without proper religious marriage papers in Pakistan. Although I had applied for divorce with Paul from afar, it would not be finalized until I had already married Shane by Islamic law at the end of my yearlong teaching contract. Shane knew that, but explained it away as a religious formality for his country.

I could not believe I was considering marrying this Pakistani Muslim. Hell, I was already married twice and was not officially divorced the second time. However, I was falling in love with his passionate soul, soulful hazel eyes and lusty good looks. I already looked forward to the next weekend.

Shane attended SGI with me and I returned the favor by attending the Muslim mosque with him. The next time I went to the mosque was to arrange for Muslim marriage. I was not ready to leave Shane. Did I really believe it would all work out? Perhaps in moments of wishful thinking, I did.

Shane's friend Nomey and my friend Song attended the 'promise ceremony.' The imam would not allow a woman to be a witness. Song gave me a colorful bouquet of daisies and purple flowers.

She said, "They remind me of you: WILD!"

I was given a list of Muslim names to choose from. I chose 'Anisah' which means 'of good company.' I liked that it sounded like anise and I loved black licorice. It was very informal with us all dressed in work casual clothes.

Nomey gave me a 14k ring with a fake ruby stone. Shane bought matching watches. Shane's dad/abu had sent a notarized letter giving legal consent for him to marry a foreigner. As I was in my 30s and had already been married and divorced, I wasn't about to play the game of seeking permission. The imam asked if he could be my 'protector,' so HE could give permission. Shane gave me $2070 for *mahr* (Muslim custom, gift for bride).

I was required to recite the *Kalimah* (sort of a declaration of being Muslim):

"Lah illa ha illallah Mohammadoor ra suh allah." It means "There is no God but Allah, and Muhammad is his messenger." Now, Shane understood I was a Buddhist. At the time I believed there was probably one God, not caring what name was given to him. My definition of god at that time was: "everything that is and isn't." I figured that Muhammad was a prophet, as there were many prophets before him in the Christian Bible. This did not deter me, therefore. Shane had high hopes and faith that I would 'see the light' and convert "from the heart" to Islam.

It's possible at a different time and place that I could have been a Muslim, had I been a Sufi. They are the esoteric Muslims: very open and nonjudgmental. They smoke a lot of weed and do a lot of singing (most beautiful *kawwalli* music), poetry writing and dancing while hanging out at shrines. They're more inclusive and loving, rather than radical *jihadi*s.

The foursome celebrated by having lunch at 'King Burger' and then Song and I went off to teach our classes at Songnam.

I had persevered throughout my very interesting but very exhausting one year contract. There were some misunderstandings on both sides, but also the Korean English teachers who had befriended me explained how unfair it was in S. Korea for employees at times.

It turned out that the Kims, in having sent me out to public schools and to another *hogwan* every week; had been getting a free foreign language teacher. They, by law, were not supposed to do that; they should have only been having me teach at THEIR *hogwan*. On the other hand, apparently many foreign ESL (English as a Second Language) teachers worked contracts on the side and made double their income.

When the Kims got greedy and I became exhausted, I gave them a copy of the law that had been printed in the English Korean paper and refused to do anymore traveling around to teach, or fill in for other *hogwans*. Enjoying the Songnam classes with Song, I did not protest those.

They used that as an excuse to fire Young, but SHE protested not getting any notice or severance and they kept her another couple of weeks. They immediately hired another teacher, a male who could NOT speak English.

I spoke with mom before leaving S. Korea. Mom said dad was still doing fine, and brother Nate sent them on Christian pilgrimage to Israel. I donated $200 spending money; Saint drove them to the airport. Later, Shane and I would send HIS parents on Muslim Hajj (pilgrimage) to Mecca in Saudi Arabia. And best of all, I would complete my own Buddhist pilgrimage in India and Nepal.

On leaving S. Korea, there were many goodbyes/gifts/meals. It was hardest saying goodbye to Song and Young. I would miss them and think of them throughout the years. Gifts were exchanged and I left them my teaching resource materials. Nomey and Shane gave me many won to hold for them.

The Kims took me to the airport, helping me with the monster bag down three flights of stairs. They paid the remainder of won for teaching; finishing out my contract. That was timely, because I had to pay $600 for having too much baggage. The Kims were shocked and dismayed that I had a ticket/visa for Pakistan. I nonchalantly said I was going to travel to several countries.

THE ADVENTURES OF A SOUTHERN BUDDHIST

Shane had gotten arrested on purpose, in order to be sent back to Pakistan. He had overstayed his visa by a couple of years. He gave all his money to me and denied having any money for fines. I bought him a one way ticket to Pakistan while buying my own ticket. I delivered it along with two new bags and a shirt, in the immigration/deportation lock-up.

I waited at the airport in Kimpo for a couple of hours before I finally saw Shane, in handcuffs (BUT not for the last time). Once we finally boarded the Korean Air plane, I switched seats with someone so we could sit together, after his cuffs were removed.

We landed in Bangkok and then several hours later boarded PIA, nicknamed "Prayers in the Air." It was a very old Pakistani plane with mostly male attendants. The two women attendants were very serious. The bathrooms got clogged less than halfway into the flight. They showed an ok American film. The evening prayers came over the intercom shortly after taking off.

I was full of trepidation and excitement to be off on another adventure; learning who I was in the world, where I fit.

How many other Americans would ever have the chance to see a Muslim country from the inside? Of course, most Americans would not be at all interested or have the courage to do such. I would be a white, American Buddhist; going to a poor, Muslim country. Oh, the things we do for love.

5. Pakistan
(Or: Bismillah, Inshallah)

Prayers in the Air took us to Islamabad, the capitol city of Pakistan. Already things had shifted again; with the first prayers and the appearance of Pakistani outfits (mostly shalwar kameez), the baggy pajama type outfits men and women wear.

The next year was to be both very dark and enlightening at the same time. That country was a sight: very dusty and dirty and dark with a harsh light. Trash was thrown everywhere. Men urinated in plain sight by the roads. Nary a trashcan was seen until I went to the US Embassy/Consulate.

Pakistan is very crowded, it smells bad (sometimes open sewage) and the traffic is scary with no one abiding by any apparent traffic rules. The buildings were old and the cars were old. There were some unique (Bedford) trucks that were all tricked out with garish decorations. The smell of gasoline and oil was powerful and made me feel squeamish.

There were hand painted billboards advertising movies. One surprising billboard was advertising birth control. Of the few women to be seen on the street, they all had their heads covered. About 5-10% had full-on burqas, with a little net window for their eyes. However, Pakistan is rather moderate, as far as Muslim countries go, so I was told.

I had a strong feeling of a big dark cloud that was descended over Pakistan. That feeling never went away until I walked over the border into India.

We were soon joined by several young men and Shane's *Mumu Majeed* (maternal uncle). We all squeezed into a tiny old car and began driving to Rawalpindi, arriving at older cousin Ghafoor and Nuzet's home. It was the top flat of a two-story home with a flat roof to gaze down at the city.

Being exhausted, bedtime came early. We had just gotten past the first loudspeaker prayer and fallen back asleep around 5:00 a.m. when the family began arriving. They began filing into the bedroom, which quickly became a sitting room. I had to escape quickly into the cold, cement-floored bathroom with cold water; high decorative cement windows open to the outside. Big fat white lizards were free to enter most rooms and they liked hiding out behind the wall-hung florescent light fixtures.

I implored Shane, "Please do not leave me alone," as I could not communicate with anyone except through sign language and smiles. He complied, being proud of his new wife. As a result, I was allowed and even expected to sit and eat with the men, getting the better portions.

That first day many family and friends arrived to pay their respects. In the afternoon Shane's parents arrived. He bowed from his waist down and touched their feet. They kissed him and hugged him. It brought tears to my eyes to see the love between them. They then turned to me.

I was introduced as Anisah, they were introduced as *Ami* (mother) and *Abu* (father). Garlands of flowers were put around Shane's neck, which he transferred to me. Ami gave Anisah/me a square gold ring with a snake on it and a yellow stone as a sun. She also gave me a gold filigree locket with a red stone in the center and a beautifully embroidered *shalwar kameez*. *Chacha* (paternal uncle) let me pick out a beautiful *shalwar kameez* when he returned from Saudi Arabia. Shane's best friend Raja gave me an expensive and fancy white *shalwar kameez,* which I picked out at their family's shop. Each shalwar kameez had a matching dupatta (big scarf/shawl).

It made me sick later when Shane left the *shalwar kameez* outfits in Pakistan when he left, along with the beautiful metal chopstick/spoon sets. He had promised to bring everything, but took it upon himself to give some of my belongings away to his female relatives.

Various people put rupees in my hand: Rs. 50, Rs. 200, Rs. 500. Rs. 50 was about $1. Meanwhile, back in South Korea the won was taking a dive. It had fallen against the dollar a bit each month when I worked there, so my salary decreased a bit each month. Shortly after Shane and I left, the bottom fell out. We had left at just the right time. Our salaries would have been half or less of the original salary when changed to dollars.

Little end tables were brought out and chai and sweets were presented. The Islamic marriage/promise certificate from Korea went around the room, along with photos taken in Korea. Shane was embarrassed that I held his arm and hand in front of his parents and he was ashamed to be going to bed with his wife while they were in the home.

Ami said, "I sleep with you?"

I was horrified and made Shane explain that American women sleep in the same bed as their husband. Apparently, married couples would often sneak out from family compounds to be together. Men often slept on the roof with other men and women slept with women. They slept on *charpai*: four-legged cots made out of wood with woven bottoms. They became couches and chairs in the day time.

Sometimes women would take me to another room and sit around me so close; touching my hair and jewelry, asking me to recite the *Kalimah*, asking to see my photos. They gave me sets of glass bangles and hennaed my hands and feet. I felt like a damn celebrity at times.

We would go to 3-day weddings, about the only kind of entertainment for women. I would be so surrounded by so many people that I felt like I couldn't breathe. My kind, oldest sister-in-law saved me a couple of times, grabbing my hand and pulling me through the crowd to a more secluded area.

One of the oddest phenomena I saw in Pakistan, and often at the weddings, was the *Hijra*. The *Hijra* is a caste of transvestites and eunuchs who dress in women's clothing. Some were hermaphrodites, some gay, and some had been kidnapped and castrated. They served a practical function. The women in Pakistan were unable to publicly dance or entertain. The *Hijra* often made their money as singers, dancers and entertainers.

Shane's family was always very sweet and kind, except for a few family intrigues and squabbles. Shane shared those in detail with me at the rented flat we had gotten. Fortunately for me/Anisah, I was not allowed to stay in the traditional family compound, as it was in an area where they made nuclear bombs. Foreigners were strictly prohibited.

We enjoyed this time: laughing, talking, playing hundreds of Scrabble games and making love. Shane got so good at spelling English words that he beat me at Scrabble a couple of times. We laughed when I admitted to cheating, to keep him from beating me.

We had another big laugh at the sight of Shane washing the big bulky, furry blanket in the old-fashioned washtub (with a washboard) in the courtyard. He looked like he was wrestling a bear, and I might near peed in my new *shalwar*, guffawing, "Shabash(well done)!"

He began teaching me the Urdu alphabet and I learned many words and phrases. I could easily greet Muslims now:

"*As-salaam Aleikum*(Peace be upon you)."

I knew what some of the main Arabic religious sayings were about: *Bismillah*—in the name of God; *Inshallah*—God willing. I often recited the Kalimah to family and friends who requested it.

One distant relative asked about the F-16 fighter jets the USA had reneged on. I had heard nothing in the USA about that issue. It took a while for me to figure out why: The Pakistanis had lied about having nuclear weapons and that had ended military and aid relief. After a very long time, the USA had finally paid back the money the Pakistani government had paid in advance for the F-16s.

The days became endless. The situation sometimes felt helpless and hopeless. The divorce stalled, and then finally came through, after several transatlantic calls and letters. For the first time, I was like a housewife with no life of my own. I cooked, because I had to be careful what I ate. I was careful to boil the water, but still got dysentery. My days were centered on reading, writing and watching tv.

The tv programs were quite an education. English CNN was on for 4 hours in the afternoon. The soaps were good and fairly easy to understand, although they generally spoke in Urdu. There were always breaks for prayer. There were many religious and music programs. I quickly grew to love the *qawwali* devotional music of the sufis, especially Nusrat Ali Fateh Khan; a national treasure. A few old American movies and series were shown, usually action or detective movies. Any time a couple kissed, it was blacked out. Any time a woman was shown with skimpy clothes, it was blacked out.

I was fascinated by the country and people. The country, in some aspects, was hell on earth. Up was down, down was up, black was white was black. The people were very hospitable one on one. Still, it felt like the Dark fucking Ages.

The Friday Times, Pakistan's first independent weekly newspaper talked about Pakistan being the 2nd most corrupt country, behind Indonesia. It was on several other "most" lists: one of the poorest, most populated, youngest, dirtiest and most illiterate.

I thoroughly enjoyed reading the newspapers and magazines of Pakistan, cover to cover. It had been surreal to see a photo of President Clinton and his family in a Korean paper, with hangul/Korean characters describing the photo. Now it was surreal to see photos of Bill Clinton with praying hands and Monica Lewinsky with a strained look on her face. This time, Urdu script writing surrounded the photos.

On the home front, the rooms were arranged around an open courtyard. The homes were secluded by a big, tall, locked metal gate at the entrance to the courtyard. The flat roofs were used to hang laundry and to sleep on. Sometimes goats were led up there with some brush, to protect them overnight. Young boys flew kites up there and men shot off weapons and fireworks on the few (mostly religious) holidays.

There was a loudspeaker positioned toward our apart. It went off at high volume before daylight every morn. On Fridays the loudspeakers all over the city would stay busy. It was their Sabbath. The sound was very eery, but I grew to appreciate deeply, the cacophony. Years later when I heard a call to prayer (*Azan*) on tv or a movie, goosebumps would arise with a shiver.

We went out at times, usually in a tiny car with several of his male family/friends. We visited other family and went to the "tourist spots." That was a laugh, because Pakistan has very few tourists since partition with India, except maybe in the Himalayan trekking region.

Shane's family was an average size: 3 brothers, 3 sisters, 20 pairs of aunts/uncles and at least 128 first cousins alone. Most of the time in his culture you married your cousin. First cousins were not off limits. While I was there, about a quarter to a half of those relatives asked Shane for money or assistance of some sort. His father, brother, uncle, cousin and various others had insisted he was to take care of them. His other responsibilities were to marry off his siblings, build another house and take care of the Toyota bus business.

I supported him emotionally and was very proud of him when he stood up to them. He told them in no uncertain terms that he had given them everything he had for a decade, never asking for anything for himself. He told them he would be independent now and they would have to take care of themselves. They would get nothing more from him. He further dictated that the remaining 3 sons could each work a decade for the family now.

In time, some of the extended family, including one brother would mouth off to Shane, telling him,

"Anisah will never take you to the US." Others tempted him, trying to get him to marry in his country. It was fairly common to have at least two wives, if a man could afford it. Most of his uncles wanted him for a son-in-law and were sorely disappointed.

I told Shane, "If you take another wife, I will take another husband."

He laughed.

Many became jealous of him and his aspirations to leave the country with his foreign wife. There were rumors of revenge and black magic.

Shane got very depressed, saying, "Korea was heaven. Now I'm in hell."

Indeed, Pakistan had so many problems. I finally decided that the population growth must be at the root, and the lack of education; along with the fundamentalism. It has got to be difficult if there are just too many people to take care of properly. At that time Pakistan was the 7th most populous country in the world. Many families had 8,9, 10 kids. The unemployment rate was super high, maybe over 60%.

Shane said, "Mom and dad have no electric, gas, tv, fridge, phone or water in their home. They have oil lamp, walk for water, cook on wood stove."

Ami couldn't read and Abu only a little, but he could speak several languages, like Shane.

There was a pretty park in Islamabad, the cleanest and friendliest city in Pakistan. Most of the consulates and embassies were there. There were some decent, small western markets there. Jinnah Market had boxes of tampons for $7. I loved to go to Islamabad and have lunch; browse through the small bookstore there. Shane, however, was usually very impatient and didn't want to waste his time nor rupees there.

A couple of times I insisted on eating at a nice restaurant. Holiday Inn buffet was $7. At Arizona Grill I ordered one of everything to ensure leftovers and it was $20. Shane refused to eat with me at those restaurants. He would go nearby to Data for Rs. 15 chicken biryani.

I loved riding the *tongas,* the cheap transportation which was a real treat for me: the horse and buggies. Shane couldn't imagine how expensive it was in the USA to ride a horse and buggy, in say, Central

Park.

One of our biggest arguments was when I bought $10 worth of books, magazines and newspapers. I insisted I had earned the dollars and won and would spend some of it, occasionally. I bought toilet paper because Shane had never used it. That was what the big plastic pitcher was for (and your left hand).

Our apart was sparsely furnished. Big long flat cushions were the couches/chairs/beds. They were where family/friends lounged and where they ate, on the floor. Shane DID buy a decent wood bed with a hidden compartment on the headboard. He kept his rupees there, from the Toyota vans he owned and ran as taxis, between Rawalpindi and Islamabad.

He didn't tell his father he was keeping money. They would settle up at the time he left for the States, and he would get his "share." His abu had worked abroad many years in Saudi Arabia. After Shane got out of the army, his abu sent him abroad to work. Shane made more money and faster in S. Korea, sending some $30,000 in just over three years to his father. The average wage in Pakistan was $50-100 per month.

He bought an ancient refrigerator which worked fine, except the electric power would often be down for hours at a time, day after day. The heater was a gas canister with the heater screwed on top—like a huge backpacker's stove. There were ceiling fans. The kitchen was a 2-burner stovetop and a small, but deep sink. It and the shower drained into a small open canal that ran along the wall and out into a bigger canal alongside the street.

When there were guests, I/Anisah insisted on making chai. Brother-in-law Javed had shown me how. It was basically loose, black Lipton tea; boiled with *dude* (milk) and *sucre* (sugar) and then strained.

Bobbi (sister-in-law) caught malaria. At the hospital it was shocking—very old everything. In the lobby was a pitcher of water with ONE dirty glass that everyone drank out of. I was never more careful to slather on OFF and thankfully never got malaria.

At the end of *Ramazan* (called *Ramadan* in other places); for *Eid -ul-Fitr* (Christmas-type holiday), many family members got in the Toyota van and went to Murree to see the snow. It's in the foothills of the Himalayas. We had fun, eating snacks and talking.

The sisters-in-law put sets of glass bangles on my wrists. They would stay there until they finally broke off, sometimes causing little cuts on my hands and wrists. Shane and I stayed while the rest of the family returned home.

We stayed in a dirty, cold (no heat) room with two twin beds and cold water only. He fought with management over a small electric heater that they charged you for, by the hour. In the morning we could still see our breath and I had 12-20 bed bug bites on my back and butt. It had been extremely noisy with truck drivers outside the window half the night.

At least Murree was nice. It had a few shops and restaurants and a chair lift to go higher into the mountains. We took a bus home.

I kept an Eid greeting card I had bought in a bookshop; for years. The front of it had a photo of a missile/rocket being launched.

It said, "Ghauri Missile(IRBM) Test, fired on 6 April 1998, at Villa Jovian(Jhelum), by Dr. AQ Khan Research Laboratories; Kahuta, Pakistan."

The inside said, "Eid greetings."

The back said, "Pakistan-The Nuclear Power of Islam, Nuclear Landmark, Chaghi(Baluchistan), 28 May 1998."

I thought it was odd that I had ended up living in two countries where there was a strong chance of a rogue nuclear disaster looming: Korea and Pakistan.

Nomie returned from Korea. He couldn't get a job after the won fell. He went out with Shane and me to visit Virsa Museum in Islamabad, and then to Faisal Mosque. It was quite opulent. The women had to go in their own section, heads covered.

Back home, the two young men laughed and joked and sang. I kept hearing a word that sounded like "banjo." I had been learning words and phrases and asked,

"What is 'banjo'?" They doubled over laughing, and Shane took me out of the room to explain,

"We were saying: '*banchod*,' which means 'sister fucker.'"

Shane and I visited Lahore (Lollywood), going to Shalimar Gardens and the Lahore Fort. We walked close to Badshahi Mosque for a glimpse.

We also visited Karachi, going to Manora Island and Clifton Beach. I was excited to ride a camel on the beach. While standing on a sea wall, a rogue wave snuck up on us, and we were drenched. We went into the KFC that had just opened with Shane's friends. I thought to myself, *I wonder what they're thinking about my wet t-shirt in this frigid air-conditioned restaurant?* My nipples were hard—I was freezing.

Karachi was where the mafia-style execution had taken place recently, of four American business men. Karachi was also the place where the journalist Daniel Pearl would be kidnapped and decapitated by terrorists a few years later.

Shane would go out daily to check on his Toyota bus business. He would bring everything I needed in the late afternoon or evening: veggies, fruit, a chicken, maybe some ground beef. Ground beef was difficult to find and they always tried to put some bones in it before they weighed it. Once while out, we chose a chicken from a small stall outside. The seller cut the neck and bled the chicken right then and there, into the open, running canal. He pulled the entire skin and feathers off in one long tug. The *dudewallah* (milk seller) would go walking up and down the narrow lanes daily, singing about his wares in a chant.

I was often alone, but didn't feel terribly unhappy. The days were monotonous, although generally pleasant enough. We would go out together about once per week. I would talk Shane into 'going out to eat,' something mostly only the men did. They called the restaurants 'hotels,' and all the waiters and cooks were male.

<hr />

AFTER THE FIRST COUPLE of weeks, I began wearing the *shalwar kameez*. It was just so much easier; less stares and attention. I had to learn it just wasn't worth it to constantly try to prove my equality and independence by looking men in the face. It became too uncomfortable and just invited trouble.

Even so, I was following Shane along a narrow, dusty walkway one day; past the little stands selling fruit, juice, and snacks. I barely glanced at a young man behind a stand. Suddenly, Shane was shouting. I didn't know what had happened until later.

Apparently, he had looked back and saw the young man reach out his hand to touch my hair. I hadn't felt a thing. Suddenly, Shane drew back his arm and slapped the man across the face, with a resounding smack. The young man had disrespected me and Shane, and Shane had to get his "honor" back. Other men standing nearby, pulled the now sobbing young man away from Shane's wrath, begging him to forgive.

That was very sobering to me and I began to understand why Shane was always so tense and impatient when we went out. Women just didn't go out much. I always wore my *dupatta* (scarf) when I went out, and it was acceptable near the capital city of Islamabad to wear it around one's shoulders. The majority covered their head, some covered their mouth too. Only a small percentage wore the *burqa*.

Another, similar episode, happened while we were sitting by the open window in our own home. We were chatting and drinking chai with our friend Raja, on the flat cushion on the floor.

There came a knock at the door. Shane began shouting. He ran out the door after a man. When he came back, he talked with the *dudewallah* (milk seller) next door.

He said, "That man thinks he is religious. He told me I should not allow my wife to sit in the window without covering her head. The *dudewallah* said he's a hypocrite and likes to stir up trouble. I told him a good religious man would not be looking in other men's windows at their women."

It was not just in MY head. The English papers in Pakistan spelled out Gloom and Doom. They were full of kidnappings, rapes, gang rapes, murder, terrorism, slavery, corruption, etc. There was constant criticism of the government, non-education, lack of rights for women and minorities...The Pakistani people are not stupid. They understand what is going on. There seemed to be a strong free press in those days.

The majority of those with means have long left the country. Since the partition of Pakistan from India 50 years ago, after a bloody Civil War, the country has never improved significantly. During the 50 year anniversary, Golden Jubilee, the people seemed to get more depressed and wondered what they had to celebrate besides the much hyped Motorway. It seemed to be the only modern highway with several lanes in Pakistan.

The new country of Pakistan had seemed full of promise. The first president, Jinnah, had declared all faiths would have equal rights. In *Curfew in the City* by Asif Farrukhi, he wrote:

'Wherever Muslims are in a minority, they become the biggest champions of secularism and of the principle that the state must treat all its citizens alike. But the attitude changes wherever Muslims form the majority community. In the latter situation, they start believing in Islamic theocracy.'

I/Anisah thought, *At least they have had a female head of government (Benazir Bhutto served as the 11th and 13th prime minister, beginning in 1988). The USA can't say that, this century.*

Later in the USA, a wonderful book was published by Greg Mortenson & David Oliver Relin in 2006: *Three Cups of Tea*. It really brings to life Pakistan and Afghanistan from a westerner's perspective.

Mortenson worked there many years building schools for children, and especially girls. He took an interest in the region after he almost got to the pinnacle of K2, the second tallest mountain in the world. He would have died if the locals had not helped him.

I could have stayed in Pakistan and never had to work again, living off of Shane's business. However, life felt very repressive and regressive in Pakistan for women, especially this western woman. The stress of dysentery again, waiting for the divorce to go through and then applying for the visa was too great.

Half the US Embassy left after the US bombed Sudan and Afghanistan, in retaliation for al-Qaeda's bombings of American embassies in Kenya and Tanzania. Americans were strongly advised to leave Pakistan. That slowed things down for a while.

WE WERE A VERY PASSIONATE couple. We loved a lot and we had explosive arguments. After a particularly bad argument in which Shane began disrespecting my religion; I began tearing up some photos and took Mohammad's name in vain, vowing to leave.

Shane slammed me to the cement floor and beat my head on it a few times. He put his big, strong hands around my throat. I couldn't breathe. I thought, *I'm going to die and go to an early grave in Pakistan. I don't want to die in Pakistan.* When he let go of my throat, I screamed,

"Help! Help!"

The young landlord's son came running down from upstairs. He refused to call the police for me (that's not a thing in Pakistan).

Shane was immediately sorry and cried and swore: "I promise I will never beat you again, so help me God."

I reminded him, "You have done the one thing I can never forgive you for. I warned you."

I walked a few miles to a travel agency in 'Pindi to get a ticket for the USA. My passport was deeply bent where Shane had tried to rip it in half.

When I returned, his family had arrived and his sweet mother began rubbing the big knots on my throbbing head, slapping Shane and crying.

The family begged me/Anisah to: "Forgive. Forgive." Shane had told me of his dad beating up his mom a time or two. He had been beside himself. He knew he was dead wrong.

I left Pakistan in a daze, walking over the border into India at Wagah. That border was often closed, due to conflict/war between the two nations that used to be one. Shane had tipped the porter, insisting to me that I not give him any more rupees.

At the border crossing, my bigass bag was emptied and everything was left in a heap for me to repack. They had tried to get more rupees from me.

I insisted: "My husband already paid him."

The border patrol said, "But you're American. You can afford it."

I, Anisah was getting weary and stated emphatically, "*Nahi*(No), not one rupee more!"

The porter carried my bag to the border and I caught a van bus with a group of mostly Koreans; to Amritsar, some 27 km (17 miles) away.

———◉———

IT FINALLY FELT AS if the dark clouds had lifted. It was uncanny, the feeling of Pakistan compared to India.

I toured the Golden Temple, the Sikhs most holy place. I had to cover my head. It was most beautiful, looking like pure gold in the sun. It was founded in 1577 by Ram Das, the fourth guru of the Sikhs. Amritsar means 'Pool of nectar,' referring to the sacred tank around which the temple is built. Part of it was built out of marble, similar to the Taj Mahal, with inlaid flowers and animals.

Their holy book, the Granth Sahib, was under a pink shroud by day; locked into an underground vault by night. There were ghoulish, bloody paintings of battles up in the clock tower museum. The Sikhs had tried valiantly to bring the Hindus and Muslims together.

I rested and had a free meal, giving a small donation. I took the Shatabdi Express the next day, to New Delhi. I visited the Taj Mahal and Agra Fort in Agra. The haunting beauty of that magical place moved me to tears.

In most photos of the Taj, one does not see the twin mosques on either side, nor the lovely river at the back. The tombs inside were sad but romantic, with the low light and the natural light coming through the lacy lattice.

Two young Indian guys asked to have a photo made with me. I didn't care. I wished many times that I had a photo of myself in front of the Taj. In those days we didn't carry phones, and I didn't have a camera.

I flew to Bangkok, Thailand next; 93% Buddhist. I luxuriated in the vibe of Bangkok. I went to the Grand Palace and several of the fantastically opulent temples: Wat Phra Keo with the Emerald Buddha; Wat Traimit with the Solid Gold Buddha; Wat Arun—The Temple of Dawn; and my fave—Wat Pho.

The Reclining Buddha resided at Wat Pho. I circumambulated and put a coin in each of the 100 offering pots. It was built by King Rama I and the first university had been there. The buddha was gold plated, 46 meters long, 15 meters high and inlaid with mother-of-pearl on the soles of the humongous feet.

I celebrated my birthday at that temple site. They taught Thai massage there, and I had a two hour Thai massage with oil and herbs for Baht 350 ($7). I also had my fortune told. Everything sounded pretty good; except one problem: love life. *Hmm...sounds true.* He said I needed a clever, charming and calm guy; ~five years older, with soul. He said my life would be easy until age 75 and that I would die at about age 87.

I went to see a new movie, *Titanic* (Paramount; 20th Century Fox).

In Thailand, one must stand for the King's Anthem, on pain of arrest. The moviegoers stood. I was enjoying the wonderful diversions and never wanted to leave. I didn't want to have to face my life back in the USA.

I returned home to SoCal in a fog. I felt like kissing the ground when I got off the plane. I had really missed the diversity of the States. In Korea 96% of the population was Korean. In Pakistan it was mostly Pakistanis, Indians and Afghanis. It was at least 95% Muslim. It had been the chance of a lifetime to feel what it was like to be a minority, and what a lesson.

I saw 1000s of USA emblems on clothing, signs, etc., in Korea. Even in Pakistan where influence from the West is frowned upon, there is a fascination of western culture, especially in more affluent circles.

In those countries, having a western education is very beneficial. Speaking English is a big advantage. English is very prolific around the world. Americans are so blessed.

———◦———

I SAW PAUL WHO WAS now living with an older female nurse. He talked a bit about getting back together, but I was done. He complemented me on my looks, saying

"You look like a model."

It must have been all that dysentery that made me lose weight, I thought. Also, I had grown out my dark hair to fit in better in Asia.

I went back to the DEEP South for a visit, worried about dad and Clay. Dad had ballooned up, looking very bloated from the prednisone. He had to lean for a while when he walked much.

I had teared up when I went with him to the flea market and he said,

"Be still a minute, Pam." He leaned on me for a few moments until he gathered enough strength to keep going.

I was shocked again when dad said, "Do you want to go to the

Chinese buffet?"

He had never liked Asian food. He had hated chicken and even turkey throughout my life, having worked as a young man for a while in a chicken factory.

He ate chicken dishes at the restaurant, saying, "I'm starved to death."

I thought, *It's the prednisone*. He talked about always being hungry.

Mom and dad showed movies of their pilgrimage and were very animated and happy and thankful for (mostly) Nate's gift. They were considering going to Ireland if dad's health improved.

It was surreal when I realized there was no more smoking in the restaurants. Philip Morris and RJReynolds were some big names I remembered seeing around the South. Big Tobacco had been sued and lost. I was very happy, being a lifetime non-smoker. I was glad, however, that mom's dad, Grandpa Roman wasn't around to see it. He had raised burley tobacco in NC for years.

Many of the relatives came to visit. Cousin Bobbie was pregnant with her 5th husband, talking about doing drugs, inviting me to join them. I regretted the one time Paul and I had smoked weed with her a few years before.

I researched "depression" for Saint, at his request. He had been accused of causing his soon to be 2nd ex-wife's depression and hospitalization. He used my knowledge, expertise and skill when it benefitted him.

On the other hand, Saint became paranoid and very angry when he saw me playing with his daughter and teaching her a couple of Korean letters, showing her how to write my name in Hangul. He provoked an argument in front of her, accusing me of trying to come between him and his daughter.

He said, "Don't believe your Aunt Pam, believe ME." He was insisting that the Korean letters might not mean what I said they did.

In essence, he had no faith or trust whatsoever in me. It was ok for HIM to try and indoctrinate Clay (and later my oldest grandson), giving him an inscribed children's bible, but it WASN'T ok for ME to be close to his daughter. He hadn't acted like that when we both had young sons of a similar age.

It got uglier and uglier, although I suggested it wasn't good to argue in front of Caitlin, who was a small child and was caught in the middle.

Caitlin said, "I don't know who to believe," sobbing.

We backed into the hallway and it escalated. The loud tones became screaming and hollering and pointing fingers. Then it got physical. I thought about calling the police on his ass, but cussed him out instead. Dad and mom arrived from church and dad got very upset, tearing up and saying,

"I wish everybody could just get along."

At that point Saint took me up on my suggestion to argue elsewhere. We went down to the picnic shed by the branch; arguing and hollering and finally calming the hell down.

Dad wanted to forget about it, also forgetting how he and his own siblings had fought over their parent's property not so long before.

Dad said, "Saint is **intolerant**." That was saying a lot, coming from dad.

I realized all over again that I had lost a brother. He cared way more about his dogmatic religious views than his relationship with his sister.

Saint said, 'You know, we're just natural enemies.'

It had not helped that mom had 'let the cat out of the bag' one evening at dinner when we were teenagers.

She had abruptly said to me, "You always WERE your dad's favorite," disdainfully. Dad, Saint and I looked at mom and each other, surprised. I had not realized it until then. Saint's feelings were obviously hurt.

Our relationship got worse after dad died. I felt like I was walking on eggshells around him and I began insisting to mom that he not be invited over *every* time I came for a visit. We began to avoid the topics of religion and politics.

I thought to myself, *I must've been a 'Holy War' Crusader or some shit in a past life!*

Clay came for a visit with a girlfriend. He had a little beard. I was so pleased to hear him call me "Mom." The whole family drove in two cars to his high school graduation. Dad insisted on paying, but I informed him that Nick owed me thousands of dollars in back support and HE should pay; which he did. Nick was now fat, balding and missing two front teeth.

Clay had big plans for going to trade school away from Nick's influence. Nick had planned out Clay's future, down to helping him build a house alongside his house. I was so glad Nick's influence was waning. Clay looked beautiful in person and in his prom picture. I was so pleased and proud. Mission accomplished!

———◉———

BEFORE I COULD GET my head on straight, the fiancé visa was approved for Shane. I was devastated. I was tormented. I vowed to myself to cancel it. I wanted to forgive, but knew when trust was broken it was usually impossible to go on.

I thought, *Maybe I could take an eye for an eye, Old Testament—Muslim style?* I loved Shane and felt really sad about never seeing his family again. They had treated me better than a daughter. I loved them and would miss them.

Shane had done the worst he could against me. Maybe if *I* did the worst thing I could against him...So when an attractive man who ran the hotel where I was staying in the city asked me to a fancy restaurant, I accepted. I knew two wrongs don't make a right, but didn't give a care. I was hungry, and not just for food. I used the nice young man for comfort and a shoulder to cry on.

I thought often of an old Spanish proverb which had been quoted by various people over the years:

99

'And God said,"Take what you will, and pay for it."' I lived by that proverb. To me, it was the very definition of karma. I tried to never do what I was unwilling to be done to me under similar circumstances; The Golden Rule, basically.

And then, the damn visa was approved and Shane was coming to SoCal. I swore I would only let him see the beautiful city and country and would then deny him and send him packing.

6. Year of Deeply Disturbing DooDoo (Or: Seven-Year Itch)

I returned to the States, mentally and emotionally kissing the ground. I had all the signs of PTSD that year and found myself getting depressed again.

It had all happened so quickly, that against my much better judgement, I married Shane. This time I married by US law in the US. Pakistan had been about Islamic law. Brother Nate, with his Taiwanese girlfriend, attended the civil ceremony at the courthouse and were witnesses.

This time, a woman married us and documented. Shane was very self-conscious when the time came:

"And now you may kiss your bride," giggling nervously to be kissing in public. This time we wore ivory colored shirts and pants. I was not thrilled, but I put up a good front. This time, we enjoyed a wonderful Indian buffet at a beautiful restaurant, rather than Burger King in Korea.

I had told Shane of the revenge: an eye for an eye; an adultery for an assault. He had been ready to go back to his country.

He was gracious and did not argue, saying, "I can tell everyone I got to the States and didn't like it."

Instead, we agreed to try and forgive one another.

———◉———

I BEGAN LEARNING TO use Nate's old computer which he gifted me. I started to study, in preparation for taking the GRE Exam. Nate had always encouraged me to go to college, and we both had undergraduate degrees.

He had asked several times, "When are you going to get your Master's?"

We, the newly married couple, stayed at a residential hotel and then got a cheap apart closer to the Mexican border.

I got a job quickly, as always, working at the county shelter. Children from infants to 18 1/2 were placed there after incidents of abuse and neglect. They were mixed in with those leaving juvie or the mental hospital. I mostly worked with the teens. My training in physical restraints was put to use, not infrequently, again.

I learned more about the world through this group of mostly underdogs: those who came from sketchy, messed up homes (if they had a home). I worked with my second unofficial sociopath—a teenage girl who tried to burn another girl up in her room, over a boy.

One night four physical restraints were taking place at once in the teen girl's cabin. The police came and several girls went away in zip-tie cuffs. It was reported in the local paper.

By that time, I had begun a Master's program in Social Work and was working the night shift. If and when the girls went to bed, I could study for a few hours in-between rounds.

———⟫◉⟪———

MOM AND DAD VISITED. Dad had been diagnosed with a rare disease—Poems Syndrome. He was now walking with a cane. A short time later he would be in a wheelchair for a couple of months and then bed bound for about eight weeks, before he died at 63. We had a sweet visit.

I said, "Mom, we should go hiking on the Appalachian Trail one of these days. We both like to walk and you're really good at hiking in the mountains."

She said, "You know I can't leave your dad."

I replied, "I'm talking about when dad is gone; something we could plan to do together in the future."

Dad said, "That sounds like a pretty good idea. You know I don't like to hike."

Mom said, "Ok, that would be fun."

I began buying matching equipment for birthdays and Christmas: boots, sleeping bags, backpacks and one-person backpacking tents.

<hr />

NEW YEAR'S, AT THE turn of the century, found me and Shane in Balboa Park, dancing in the rain. Shane was bemused by my public display of joy. He was working under the table at a new Palestinian friend's chicken restaurant. He began studying at the nearby, free community college. I taught him how to drive a straight shift car on the freeways, making up for not having to teach Clay.

One day after an argument, I had a sudden urge to look through Shane's things, and found a stash of thousands of dollars he had hidden in the closet. I was incensed and very suspicious. We had just sent $5000 to Pakistan for his parent's Hajj to Mecca. I opened a new savings account in my name only and deposited the cash.

Shane was beside himself when he learned of the new account without his name. He literally jumped up and down and I laughed at him. HE was now at the mercy of someone in a foreign country and culture.

I questioned him, "Why would you hide money from your wife?"

He said, "I was saving it for my Palestinian friend. It's not mine."

I allowed him to save all his money until he had almost the same amount that I had confiscated, while I paid all the bills. Shortly after that he raised his hand as a threat to me, during yet another argument.

About a year had gone by in the States, and I received a letter from the young man I had dated briefly, for revenge. I don't know how he got my address, but there it was. He had been concerned and asked how I was doing. The thing is, I had sincerely liked him and had wondered all year if I had done the right thing. He had begged me to cancel Shane's visa.

I knew that it was only a matter of time before I would leave Shane, and I told him as much. The hidden stash of cash and the threat had clinched my decision. I would decide when, where and how; at MY convenience. I wrote Brendon back.

———————●———————

DAD DIED THREE WEEKS after a visit back to the DEEP South. He was bed bound, but happy to visit. One of my favorite memories was sitting in a rocking chair with my 2nd grandchild in dad's room while everyone else had gone out to dinner. When the baby cried, dad just smiled peacefully. In the past, that would have bothered him greatly.

Clay had gotten very busy after his high school graduation. He married an older woman he'd only dated a couple of months. She had a young son and they soon had a daughter together, and now a son; all within about 2 years. I had not been invited to the wedding, but it sounded like they had practically eloped, going to a wedding chapel in the Smokies. I gave him a new computer for a wedding present. It was still uncommon in those days to own a PC (personal computer).

I saw the generational pattern play out: Mom had me at 18, I gave birth to Clay at 19, his firstborn came when he was 19. I was a grandmother at 39. Mom was a great grandmother at 58. Clay would become a wonderful parent, in my eyes; but that would not stop one of his oldest kids from distancing from him (and the rest of the family) some years later, after their parent's divorce.

A whole era had ended. My biggest ally in the family was gone and everything shifted. Although dad was a traditional, conservative "Archie type," he had instilled strength and worthiness into me. He loved me better than most had in this life. He held back a good bit of the family dogma to protect me and he had learned to be tolerant. He even had an atheist friend the last few years of his life.

He had cried and told me, "I'm afraid I won't see you again."

I reassured him, "I really believe we will be together again, Dad. You know we are ALL betting our lives on our firm belief in a life after this one. We both have to lean on our sincere faith."

Dad nodded, and seemed to be at peace. I firmly believed we WOULD see each other again (although I thought to myself that *it might not be in Christian Heaven, but in another life*).

Dad cried again while begging each family member in turn, "Please forgive me if there is anything I have done to you."

I said, "Dad, anytime I had a problem with you, I confronted you with it. I have no resentments. We're good. I love you."

"I love YOU," Dad said.

Brother Saint chose that time, with dad on his deathbed, to be forthcoming. When asked, he told dad he thought that he had been abusive towards mom. He had cowardly said nothing all the years when it might have made a difference in dad's demanding and dismissive attitude towards mom.

Dad was ready to die and didn't want to live as an invalid, dependent on mom. He had never cried more than once or twice in my life until he got sick. He cried frequently after that, becoming emotionally mature.

I asked him, "Would you like me to say a special prayer so you can die?"

He thought a moment, and said, "I would appreciate that."

That made ME tear up, because I felt validated, as if my Buddhist prayers counted/mattered. When I returned home, I did a special sadhana, praying for his peaceful death. Three weeks later, it worked. Nate bought us tickets to fly back out for the funeral together.

I saw Clay at the funeral. Someone asked if we were brother and sister. He watched as I threw a rose into dad's grave, and he did the same. I felt euphoria for the next few weeks, happy that dad had gotten his wish. I was happy for him that he no longer had to suffer this life.

That next year, however, would be a blur of grief and Master's program. When I was home, the river of tears would flow. They were endless. It was a deep well of hurt and loss. It took my breath away. Fortunately, I was able to pour myself into my work and studies, otherwise.

Mom came out to visit that spring and I took her on a roadtrip to see the Grand Canyon, her first time. We stayed over in Vegas, and I gambled my designated $20 and had two drinks. Mom didn't drink or smoke or curse and neither had dad. However, she didn't object to my drinking and gambling, in moderation.

We viewed Hoover Dam on the way, getting out of the car to marvel at that great engineering feat. I remembered my first time seeing the canyon. I had to sit down. The vastness and contrast of the canyon walls made me dizzy.

The Grand Canyon was enticing, and we decided on a hike to the bottom, utilizing Bright Angel Trail. It was the end of May and it was hot. We took water bottles and protein bars. We had on hats and we walked down at a steady pace, switchback after switchback, stopping at the 1.5 mile rest house to get more water. We stopped at the 3 mile rest house to fill up again. By the time we made it down to Indian Garden, it was 108 degrees.

The sun was not visible down *IN* the canyon, except for a few hours around noon. You had to look up to see the strong light. I had to lie down. I was exhausted. My face was red and I felt very weak. Mom seemed to be okay. I kept sipping water in the shade. The shadows above the canyon warned of night coming. It was getting a bit cooler, with a little breeze.

Mom said, "It's getting late. Are we going to sleep here tonight?"

I said, "Let me sit up and see how I feel."

She found a walking stick for me, and I got up off the canyon floor and sat on a bench. I was finally able to stand up and walk slowly. Little by little my stamina came back and I got my second wind.

Going up was, of course more difficult, but my knees liked going up better than going down. We had to stop frequently; now mom was getting exhausted. Just as it was getting rather hard to see, the full moon rose over the canyon. It was awesomely magical.

We walked ten minutes, paused, walked ten minutes, paused. I warned her, "Look out for that rock, it moved. There's a little hole—don't trip. Step down here."

We finally climbed out of the canyon at about 10:00 p.m. We found food at a gas station on the way to our isolated motel. We were very hungry, but even more tired, collapsing into our beds.

The next morning, mom said, "Look at this!"

I looked, and said, "Me too!"

We discovered that we each had a big toenail and a little toenail that turned black. That adventure gave us courage later, on the Appalachian Trail.

AFTER A FEW LETTERS back and forth, I began secretly seeing Brendon again, just before the Twin Towers were hit in NYC on 9/11. I was on my 2nd day of internship at a hospice. As I was driving to the internship, I heard the news on the radio of the first crash. As I was listening to the broadcast, the other plane hit the other tower. Everyone was talking about it at work and all the televisions were tuned to the terrorist events at hand, in the homes we visited.

I immediately called Shane and warned him, "Please do not speak with anyone about the attack. You are Muslim—you will definitely be at risk of being a target now."

We stuck a big American flag sticker on the window of the apart when I got home.

Shane often passed himself off as Hispanic after that, much as I had passed as Afghani or Irish in his country when there were extremists around. It was purely for safety.

I felt a great shock and sadness, along with the whole country. The USA came together as one, in order to mourn the lost and to defend itself. I also felt a deep sadness for the Muslim folks I knew personally. I knew many of them were good people who loved Americans and would give anything to move here for the opportunities. I foresaw the discrimination they would face after 9/11. I thought, *I'm glad dad didn't have to live through this.*

Shane began to suspect I was leaving, especially when the apartment got emptier and emptier. I had told him I wouldn't stay with him after I found the stashed cash and he threatened me.

Brendon and I got two studio apartments in the same building, different floors. I continued to pick up my mail, at now Shane's apartment. My name had been taken off the lease. We would go out for a meal together and talk.

I hoped to remain friends. He had come to the USA for me. I knew how difficult it was to be in a foreign country alone and, after all, I was legally responsible for him. However, it was impossible not to argue at times. One afternoon after a heated argument; he said, "I'll kill you."

I had warned him, but he couldn't understand. He followed me to the post office, where I had gone to change my mailing address. A nice, older black man overheard us arguing. I was self-conscious of all the people in line and whispered loudly,

"Please leave. I don't want to talk to you. I told you I'd call the police if you followed me."

He said, "I'll wait for you outside," and exited.

The nice black man behind me asked me discreetly, "Are you okay?"

I felt my face get red hot. Tears slid down my face, unbidden. "No," I said.

It had come down to *this*. I had worked and volunteered with battered women. It was time to take care of myself.

He said, "Do you want me to call the police? I'll wait with you until they get here."

I thought about it briefly: *I have to nip this in the bud. He already beat me up once, raised a hand, and now he has threatened me. I am no longer in Pakistan—I am safe now, to stand up to him. I need to handle this once and for all.*

I nodded. The nice man waited with me about 10 minutes until the police arrived, blocking both the entrance and exits.

When the police walked up to his old van, the look on Shane's face was PRICELESS, as it dawned on him he had no control over the situation. He went away in cuffs, looking sheepishly into my eyes. HA.

I wanted to say, "Allah Akbar(God is Great)," but restrained myself. Blamed if he knew what had happened to him! The police report said he had made 'terrorist threats.'

Shane had someone else bail him out, as I refused when he kept calling me. I immediately filed for divorce and a three year restraining order was ordered for protection against him. Brother Nate stood by my side as usual; figuratively, and literally in court.

Shane quickly married a divorced, white Muslim woman with two daughters and moved to Texas. He was not heard from again. Not until after the three years restraining order had expired, at least.

Finally free, I could breathe again. I'd experienced some of the worst events a person can live through in the past year: getting beat up in a foreign country by someone you loved; death of a beloved father; and a terrorist attack on our beloved nation. It was a wonder I wasn't in the f'n loony bin.

It took some time, but I realized that the most beautiful thing I would take from my third marriage was the experience of living in three very different countries with someone from a different world. Once again, I forgave when I left. The resentments quickly melted away. I would hold on to the good and let go of the tragedy. I would overcome, eventually.

THE WONDERFUL OFFSET to that disturbing time was the successful completion of my Master's degree. I now had legal letters after my name: MSW. Masters of Social Work. The hospice where I did my internship hired me; a goal I had been shooting for. I poured myself into school and career as I continued to mourn. That first year had felt like a tsunami washing over and sweeping me underwater.

The hospice patients and their families were from every walk of life. It was so interesting to visit a poor home in a shabby apartment in the city and then cross the Coronado bridge and visit in a big "old money" home. I was assigned the hospice's five hospitals initially, and grew accustomed to navigating the hospital systems and staff.

It was fascinating sitting in IDG (Interdisciplinary group) and listening to the MDs, RNs, chaplains, MSWs, aides and volunteers report on patients. I became proficient at giving my own reports from MSW perspective. I loved being part of a team. One of the doctors recommended me to lead the IDG, which I did successfully for more than a year.

At the beginning of my hospice career of 20 years, I charted in physical paper charts. By the 2nd year I was assigned a laptop and we were taught a medical program which we charted on. It was in the days of dial up, but it was so nice to be able to chart from home and synchronize notes to the hospice. Throughout my career the medical programs changed several times. I picked it up fairly easily, thanks to Nate giving me his old computer to practice on. Many on the medical teams had trouble with electronic documentation.

I loved driving around, often long distances, to visit our patients and families. It was an easy way to learn the counties I worked in, with all of the back and side roads. Dad had taught me long ago how to read a map and I always had my trusty *Thomas Brothers* map book with me. When the GPS and smartphones became common, it was only when a proper map book couldn't be found that I decided to switch.

I settled into my new career and with my new boyfriend. We had so much fun, eating at just about every nice restaurant downtown. I even bought designated "margarita drinking shoes," to party in. He was a trained *sous* chef, and like mom, could turn out delightful meals with great aplomb and mastery. The difference was his cooking was sophisticated and geared to a low carb diet which I preferred. Mom's style was down-home, country cooking with some experimentation; high sugar and carb with lots of desserts.

He bought me a bouquet of flowers weekly throughout our years together. A guy at the flower shop said,

"You must stay in the 'doghouse' a lot, you buy so many flowers."

Brendon said, "No, I'm in love."

In a short time we were engaged. He was to become the next "husband of the decade." Brendon gave me a stunning one-carat ring, that I picked out, a first for me.

Brendon was nice looking, having the slicked back hair of an Italian/Irish and being tall and slim. He reminded me of the character actor Dean Winters, who played in the *Oz* series on HBO. He always took care of me in ways I wasn't used to. He would take care of things, just because he knew they needed to be done. He spoiled me, as mom said. We were passionate and loving.

I excelled at hospice social work and was now making double the income, with better benefits. We had good health insurance. My coworkers were interesting and fun. It was a whole new world.

———◉———

MARRIAGE #4 TOOK PLACE on a cruise ship sailing to Alaska, presided over by the Captain of the ship. We warmed up the beautiful little chapel for three other couples that got married that day. It was an exquisite adventure, and we had beautiful photos made to commemorate the day.

We did the Inside Passage, getting out at quaint and rustic ports. We saw many eagles cruising the skies as we cruised into the Juneau port. We took a helicopter to the top of Mendenhall Glacier.

I would never forget the creaks and groans as that living, frozen body of water moved by infinitesimal amounts. We were able to get some glacial water in a soda bottle which we took home and poured into a beautiful decanter.

We saw so many waterfalls, glaciers and seals. We saw a glacier calve into the sea, creating an iceberg at Tracy Arm Fjord. It was otherworldly: the bright, dark turquoise color. It was cold out on our balcony and we ordered hot Kahlua coffee and wrapped up in a blanket as we enjoyed the long show going by slowly.

At one of the last ports—Victoria Island, B. C.; the Canadian Mounties came to the newlywed's cruise ship door. They came in and made Brendon and me stack all our luggage and belongings into the narrow hallway while they searched the room. Other guests were passing by us in the cramped hallway, getting ready to disembark, and they stared at the spectacle.

The policeman said, "Sir, we found some cocaine residue on your CADL. We checked, because your name came up in our database as a felon with a crack cocaine charge. You will not be allowed to disembark."

I was mortified. However, I stayed in solidarity with him, eating on the ship instead of having the scrumptious high tea that had been planned on Victoria Island.

Brendon swore, "It is mistaken identity. There is another guy with the same name they are confusing me with."

He had already told me he had dabbled with drugs; we had talked about experimenting with drugs, but nothing so addictive. He had told me he had a misdemeanor when he was a minor. I chose to believe him, although devastated and embarrassed. We were already married, after all, having dated a year. I had DONE a background check on the internet when we began dating. I had learned to be more careful in my choice of partners, but nothing had shown up on the check.

I had another moment of pause when I paid the final bill for the cruise. There were many alcoholic drinks I had not known about. We had both had a couple drinks per day, this was well beyond that. There were also gambling charges I had not known about. I had a bad feeling in my gut, but what was done was done. Brendon worked hard, and we paid off the credit card for our wedding trip quickly.

Some of the best days of my life were ahead. The hospice job fed my soul. I excelled and made good friends. Nate and I visited frequently and would go out sailing on his boat. Sometimes we'd just sit at dock in the marina and drink hot tea in the cabin.

We went out for longer trips, out of the bays and past Point Loma, into the Pacific. It felt very freeing with the wind in one's face, watching the waves go under. It was fun when a seal or sea lion came up close. We would float and watch the fireworks from SeaWorld practically fall on us. We sailed out past the US into the waters of Mexico.

I began to take in the sights around the extended west, going up Highway 1 and going out into the mountains and deserts. I timed it so I could be in the desert during a butterfly migration. The air was thick with them! I couldn't walk without touching them. The blooms in late winter in the desert were so lovely. I had not realized how much bloomed in the desert.

I would visit many national parks: Death Valley, Joshua Tree, Yosemite, Sequoia, Grand Canyon, Yellowstone...They were sensational and peaceful (if you went off season). Sometimes I went alone, longing for adventure and solitude.

I would walk over the border into Mexico alone. I could get away with being seen as a local if I didn't wear designer clothes or expensive jewelry and kept my mouth shut. I'd tuck my money and ID into a pocket. I'd been able to pass as an Afghan in Pakistan, wearing a *shalwar kameez* with *dupatta* and my hair down, not peering into eyes of those around me. Again, I had to keep my mouth shut.

I CONTINUED TO ATTEND SGI and to contemplate karma and past lives and how they intersected with this life. I visited Deer Park Monastery in Escondido. It was established by the late, great Thich Nhat Hanh: a famous Vietnamese monk who had championed civil rights for his people. He became famous in the West for his teachings and books, such as: *No Mud, No Lotus*. He was of the Zen tradition.

I enjoyed the beautiful and serene surroundings and found it very interesting to meditate in silence and to eat with others in silence. I was used to public and private chanting and that helped me to focus and concentrate.

I read the new book that came out by Paramahansa Yogananda(all 1696 pages and 75 chapters): *The Second Coming of Christ; The Resurrection of the Christ Within You; A revelatory commentary on the original teachings of Jesus.* It cemented what I had been thinking about Christ Jesus and The Gospels. I especially loved the artist drawing of Jesus in a meditation position.

Living in SoCal, S. Korea and Pakistan gave me a sense of the world. I had studied Cultural Competency in Social Work classes; but really learned it in my jobs, relationships and travels.

I realized how much living abroad had changed me. It had been a helluva education, alongside my degrees. It had given me a world view and forever changed the way I looked at things. The things people turned their nose up at: a bad sewage system, trash/garbage on the street, a dirt floor in a home, or the smells of a live food market/farm; was not catastrophic to me. I had a much higher tolerance level than most people I knew.

I often thought I would love to be on a spaceship to look at beautiful planet Earth from space; to get an even deeper perspective.

Those experiences made me more empathetic and wise. At the same time, I became more ostracized. I was now seen as more of an outsider in the fundamentalist/evangelical communities of the DEEP South. I could only fit in if I kept my mouth shut and pretended; but I wasn't a poser. I could only be who I am. I would advocate for ME the way I advocated for all our patients, families, clients.

It was still hurtful, but it made me stronger. I was learning Patience from my fundamentalist family, and especially from Saint. They were helping me become a better person.

Mom would say, "I'm praying for you."

I told mom, "Thank you for all your prayers. Your prayers have helped me find My Path." She wasn't exactly happy: SHE wanted a different path for me.

———◉———

BRENDON AND I FOUND a small Spanish style house close to downtown which we loved. We would live there for several years. We even tried to have a baby for a little while. However, after an argument of some seeming insignificance, Brendon disappeared for a few days. This had happened once before, but while we were dating and living in separate apartments.

I got worried for his safety after trying to call him for a couple of days. I called his boss at the restaurant and found out he hadn't been going to work. I then talked it over with one of my friends and decided to check the police records; run a check downtown. Sure enough, Brendon's name came up for a crack cocaine charge. He had been forced into a halfway house for rehabilitation for six months, a few years ago.

I packed all his shit, placing it by the door for him. He came home the fourth day, full of lies and bluster.

I asked him, "Where have you been?"

He said, "I just didn't want to come home when you pissed me off."

I laid the court reports in his lap and asked,

"What about these? You may as well tell me the truth, I already know what you're about."

When he knew he was busted, he came clean and humbled himself, saying, "I've been staying at a hotel doing cocaine."

I asked, "Doing cocaine or smoking crack?"

He said, "Smoking crack."

I said, "Why did you come home now?"

He said, "I came home when the money was gone."

He had overdrawn the bank accounts, going through all the money and more. He was blacklisted by ChexSytems, and he couldn't get a bank account for some years after.

I asked him what else he had lied to me about, and he began to tell me as I questioned him: "I do *not* have a college degree. I do *not* have a daughter. I DO have a felony conviction. I DO have addiction issues."

I said, "I'm going to check if you have a record back east in your former city. I actually did a general background check online when we started dating, but nothing came up. Is there anything else you're keeping from me?"

He said, "I am still paying off court ordered restitution back east, where I stole from a restaurant I worked at, before I moved across country."

I asked, "How much did you steal?"

He said, "Thousands of dollars."

It all came together for me in my mind, and I said: "So the Canadian police were right about you on our honeymoon."

He nodded his head. He had known I would never marry him if I knew he had drug addiction issues, knew he was a felon. I had *worked* at a drug rehab and knew how easy it was to relapse. In my heart, I knew it would not last. It wasn't just the drugs or even the theft: it was ***the lies again***.

I immediately went back on the pill, although sex was the furthest thing from my mind for a while; a child with him was completely out of the question. To Brendon's credit, he went to a psychiatrist for a few months and began AA meetings, going regularly.

I stayed for a time while it played out. We still loved each other.

Love for me never died immediately. The heavy feeling in the pit of my stomach returned, knowing another relationship was doomed to fail. I again saw the karmic pattern playing out, related to deception.

I prayed, "May no one ever suffer the pain of deception."

———————⊙———————

AT A REGULAR PHYSICAL it was discovered that my left ovary was much enlarged. The PSA test came back elevated.

I explained the symptoms and tests and asked our hospice physician, "What are my aunt's chances?"

He said (not realizing it was ME), "Her chances are not good if it's ovarian cancer. Usually by the time it is detected, it is advanced cancer with a prognosis of about six months to a year."

I had been working with the dying for a couple of years by now and knew how to make preparations to die. I knew how to talk with doctors and nurses. I had read *No More Hysterectomies* (by Vicki Hufnagel, M.D. with Susan Golant) and had been planning to get a uterine fibroid embolization to stop the heavy bleeding I had been experiencing for a few years now. I had gotten anemic at one point, 'seeing stars' while walking up stairs. It had probably been part of the reason I'd collapsed in the Grand Canyon.

However, they were going to have to cut me open to remove my ovary. I decided to go ahead and get a supracervical hysterectomy and a left oomphorectomy; leaving my cervix and good ovary. Most of the time in those days, they just snipped everything out.

I had heard stories nurses told about prolapsed uteruses and vaginas and even bladders. I looked younger than my years and sex was important to me. No, thank-you: I would not maim myself unnecessarily.

Fortunately, I had good health insurance and good care at a women's hospital nearby. It was not cancer. I began to have more energy than I'd had in years. Mom came out to care for me while Brendon worked. Nate came over almost every day.

Brendon and I began talking about moving back to the East coast. I had been a resident of California for 12 years, if you included the two years abroad. My son, mom and grandkids were far away. The cancer scare had been the deciding factor.

I didn't really WANT to move back to the DEEP South, but it was time to live closer to my other family. I didn't want to leave California or Nate, but felt I must. Brendon's family lived back east, too. Thus far I had lived in a different state each decade: Illinois, Georgia, N. Carolina and California.

I felt a little bit better knowing that Nate was dating a nice Hispanic/Latina woman I had introduced him to. We worked together at the hospice. He wouldn't be alone.

Mom and I decided we would do our hike on the Appalachian Trail before I went looking for a job in NC. Brendon would find us a place to live and get a job, in the meantime.

A few months before we moved, we adopted a beautiful and whimsical doggy from the Humane Society. She was half St. Bernard and half blue-tick coonhound. She would ride across country, almost 2000 miles with us. Bigass, lapdoggy Ziggy took the place of a child for us.

7. Appalachian Trail, an Adventure Travelogue

Mom and I began in earnest, planning our hike. I did most all of the early planning: buying the guides, maps, boots, tents, sleeping bags, backpacks and backpacking stove. My favorite piece of equipment was the titanium spork. Although mom was interested, she was mainly along for the ride. She liked the idea of spending quality time with her daughter after her husband died.

I studied like I was in college: reading books, going online. I even read *A Walk in the Woods* by Bill Bryson and *Wild* by Cheryl Strayed, before they became movies. The books are always better. I subscribed to *Backpacker* and *Outside* Magazines for a couple of years, getting valuable tips and inspiration. I got a little Campmor catalog and ordered many things. They were more reasonably priced in those days.

We were both familiar with the mountains, having lived in them many years: the sunset over the mountain, the sunrise over the mountain, the storm coming over the mountain, the mountains encircling the lake, the mountains encircling the town, the need to go up/down/up/down and swerve to the left, swerve to the right around curve after curve while driving...

The A.T. touched the county mom lived in and other surrounding counties. There were at least three points where there was access, near the house dad built. Most people would begin at the southern terminus, at Springer Mountain in Georgia. They would begin when it was still cold, just before spring. A few would make it to the northern terminus in Maine on Mt. Katahdin before winter.

However, all the articles emphasized doing your own hike. What made sense to ME was to begin just over the Virginia line and head south. I had no illusions of completing the entire trail in one year, making an arbitrary goal of 500 miles. That too would remain illusive, but over time I would make it happen.

The floors of mom's house became covered with piles of hiking things. There were lists to check and recheck. Eureka Backcountry I tents were set up and taken down and set up again. Kelty Haiku backpacks were adjusted. Kelty Light Year 3D sleeping bags were tested and then stuffed in their sacks. The MSR Pocket Rocket stove was tested outside. Waterproof covers were tested. Mountain House freeze dried meals, little packages of food, drink mixes, jerky and trail mix was divided into two piles. Iodine "pills" (as mom called them) would purify the water we would find as we hiked along.

Two resupply boxes were prepared. Brendon would be the support person. He had given me the requested orange Leatherman Juice multi-tool pocketknife for Christmas, although he was opposed to me being gone for weeks.

He dropped us off in the town of Damascus, Virginia, in late spring of '05. Our packs were HEAVY. I had tried to keep the weight down, but realized in hindsight why people take too much as beginners. The weight of STUFF on the back of a beginner backpacker is a security blanket. We just don't realize how little we actually need.

Mom had made brownies and we stuffed those in foil, into our already-full packs. I velcroed on the dual action Cho-Pat knee braces, which would become part of my daily attire. My Columbia floppy hat (with netting poked inside, which kept insects and mice at bay in the shelters) went on last.

After goodbyes with Brendon and Ziggy doggy, we went up, uP, **UP** the mountain from the cute little trail town. I felt a bit overwhelmed, being in the middle of the woods up in the mountains with only a backpack, but put on a brave front for mom's benefit.

I quoted the beginning of a Walt Whitman poem:
Song of the Open Road

Afoot and light-hearted I take to the open road.
Healthy, free, the world before me,
The long brown path before me leading wherever I
choose.
Henceforth I ask not good-fortune,
I myself am good-fortune.
Henceforth, I whimper no more, postpone no more,
need nothing.

Poetry made us think of Grandma Della, and then we thought about dad's sister Jo, who had just died. We wondered if maybe it was possible for our dead relatives to see us out in the woods from a vantage point, perhaps from up in heaven.

We were 'give out' before too long. It was already late in the afternoon and we had already travelled from Georgia. We found a mostly level spot and set up our tents, side by side. We had hiked five miles. We were in Tennessee.

The plan had been to get in shape ON the trail. Mom gained a lot of weight being a caregiver for a decade for both grandmothers, and then dad. *She needs this, whether she realizes it or not,* I thought.

I was also recovering: from surgery and from all the betrayals. The latest betrayal being a crackhead, felon husband who told lies.

My feelings about the mountains were evolving. I had felt trapped after first moving to the DEEP South. Surely the molestation from Chester had added greatly to that feeling. I remembered being a teenager, sitting in a booth at dinner time at my workplace: Ok's BBQ. "Freebird" (by Lynard Skynard) played on the jukebox, and I gazed down the main road with no stoplights, dreaming of the day I would leave the mountains forever.

I went to Denver at 18 on my first airplane trip, and then to Estes Park by bus. It was for a teen retreat, a camp for the church youth. I was wowed by the Rocky Mountains. When I returned home, there was a little bit of appreciation for the Blue Ridge Mountains now.

I had hiked with Song in South Korea to the top of Hallasan where you could see a bit into the extinct volcano. I had driven up into the mountains to touch snow at Death Valley NP. I was determined now, to make peace with the Appalachian Mountains.

⎯⎯⎯◉⎯⎯⎯

THE SECOND DAY ON THE AT, I heard a commotion and turned my head to the right, looking down the mountain. A big black bear galloped up through the woods close to me. I was up on the trail which was sort of a ledge, looking down. As soon as the bear saw me, it wheeled around and headed back down the mountain. I was frozen in awe for a few moments. Remembering, I reached into the backpack side pocket to touch the large bear spray canister. I practiced drawing it, like a gun.

I figured now would be a good time to test the whistle around my neck. Mom had one too. She came around the bend shortly, but missed the bear. She didn't care. She had bears come out of the woods to eat out of the garbage cans at her house. She'd bring the cans into the basement for a few days and they'd move on. Her dog treed a cub once and it wouldn't come down until the dog was put in the basement. Dad made a video. The cub jumped down and then back into another tree. It had looked almost like a monkey, the way it maneuvered.

By the 3rd or 4th day, mom said, "I don't care if we go home, anytime; if you want. We've already been out here longer than anyone thought we would."

I replied, "You can if YOU want, but I'm staying."

Mom said, "Well I'm not going to leave you out here by yourSELF."

Mom had asked me before we took off, when she was sure we were really going, "Is it ok if Saint goes?"

I said, "No! This is a mother/daughter thing. If he goes, I'm not going."

I had done all the planning and buying for the trip. I'd be damned if she'd let Saint take over and ruin everything now. She was so used to having a man in charge her whole life, that she couldn't imagine two women alone in the woods for weeks.

We had many a talk going up and down and up and down and around the mountains. We began with dad, and mom's feelings about how he had treated her. I felt like I was becoming mom's therapist. That was fine to a point, but this was **dad** we were talking about. I had to draw a boundary line—asking mom,

"Please don't talk bad about dad to me anymore. Maybe you could talk about those feelings with your siblings or friends, instead. And please, don't expect me to put up with Uncle Bryce 'giving him down the road' anymore, especially in the house dad built for us."

I talked to dad when he was alive and well and had told him how I felt about his treatment of mom. A few times. Mom refused to stand up for herself and/or leave. Of course, she stayed because there weren't many options in those days for divorced, religious women. She never worked outside the home more than a couple of years in her life.

However, dad was dead. He was my beloved father. I would not hear anything against him for long. He could not defend himself. I loved them both and fought as an adult to forge a relationship with them both, that was real.

Mom and dad loved each other. They both said so. In the will dad wrote, and everybody (Mom, Saint, Nate and I) agreed to, he wrote in words that mom was his equal partner in life. That always made me tear up. I had fond memories of mom sitting in dad's lap in the living room. Once as small children, Saint had sneaked up the stairs to their room to "scare them." He had come back down and whispered to me about seeing them naked, with dad on top of mom.

I said, "I've had several dreams about dad."

Mom said, "Were they good?"

I began to share the dreams I'd had about dad since he died.

"In the first dream, I'm sitting in the car with you. I see dad, you don't. You remind me that he's dead. Dad and I give each other a knowing look."

Mom smiled.

"In the second dream, dad's going up in an elevator. I say, 'Hi! Hi! Hi!', bending down to see him a little longer."

I make the motion of bending down and waving. Mom smiled again.

"In the third one, I'm in a stadium. Dad is in the stands watching me perform, kind of like when I was in band (but he missed most of those performances)."

Mom said, "Yeah, he was usually working. I think he regretted not spending more time with you kids after he got sick."

I continued, "In the fourth one, I was so upset about Shane beating me up and was wondering what I should do (mom and I had talked at length for the first time about that on the A.T.). He just looks me in the eyes and gives me a long hug."

I broke up and a tear slid down my face.

Mom said, "I'm sure glad you're not in Pakistan anymore. We worried about you being so far away in a 'Moslem' country."

I wiped my cheek and said, "I'm relieved that's all behind me now. I had one last dream about dad recently. In the dream he's standing on the corner, waiting for the bus which I'm on. I see him and get off the bus. Everyone on the corner is dad! I look up into many faces, and they're all dad."

Mom said, "That's strange..."

I said, "You know how dad had a funny sense of humor-in four of the five dreams, there's a sense of humor. So like dad."

I took to saying, "Our Father, who art in Heaven..." when speaking of dad to my siblings. Nate got it, Saint not so much. Dad was probably laughing his ass off somewhere.

Mom was glad I had lovely dreams to help me grieve. She had had a couple of dreams herself.

Dad had told her, "I love you." The best dream of all, she'd turned over in bed and he was there. He had his young body again.

I was able to hash over old hurts with mom on the trail. I told her how I'd felt when she favored Saint over me, favored his kids over mine. How their extremism had turned me away. How I wasn't to blame because Chester molested me. Mom expressed genuine remorse.

I apologized for the times I had given mom a hard time. Our relationship grew stronger. Mom became my friend and I could depend on her in the future.

We gossiped about all the relatives and family friends. I analyzed them all for her, an old game from when I was a pre-teen, dreaming of being a psychiatrist.

Mom told me about Bob & Betty's daughter Deena, borrowing money from them a couple of times. She had paid it back. After dad died, she had wasted no time asking mom to borrow more money. She did NOT pay it back for a very long time—much longer than she had promised. The gossip in the family was that she liked to gamble. At the very least, she usually lived beyond her means, trying to impress everyone.

I said to mom, "You have to promise to never loan her money again."

I was incensed; ready to blow up the family over this potential abuse of a widow on a fixed income.

She said, "Oh alright, I promise. You don't have to cause a commotion in the family."

Mom kept her promise and refused to loan any more money to Deena the next time she asked, and she DID ask again.

Mom confessed she had changed the will that we had all agreed to when dad was alive. She changed it at Saint's whining, to his advantage. He even suggested to mom later that maybe brother Nate should be left out of the will altogether. I expressed my complete disapproval of that selfish plot.

Periodically, over the years, mom would ask me if I minded if she changed something else to benefit Saint. He wanted his share of the property now, with the pretext of saving mom taxes, for example.

I would reply, "Yes, I mind." Saint didn't have the balls to question dad, but would continue to whine about how he deserved more, to mom who had often favored him. Perhaps she felt guilty, since dad had questioned (*wrongly*) if Saint was his son. *Men.* Mom might have her faults, but being a liar or cheater wasn't one of them. I never knew her to ever lie about anything, if asked directly.

———— ◉ ————

OUR ROLES CHANGED ON the trail. At mom's house, she was the queen of the kitchen. I washed the dishes and cleaned up. On the trail, I heated up our food on the backpacker stove. I made the coffee. Mom washed the little titanium pans and Nalgene water bottles and utensils.

We took turns getting water. When we'd arrive at a shelter there would usually be a stream nearby. Sometimes it was downhill after walking all day. If it was a spring, we figured we didn't have to filter. If it was a stream, we always filtered.

We never camped near a road or small campground. We had heard a couple of stories about someone getting killed on the trail, but it was usually near a road. Most people would not hike miles up a mountain to hurt other people. Psycho-killers seemed to be more opportunistic.

The camaraderie on the A.T. was phenomenal. We met so many nice, unusual and weird people. For example, there was Mousetrap, who carried a couple of mousetraps with him and would set them up around his sleeping bag in the shelters. We woke up a couple of times that night, to the sound of "SNAPPp."

We almost never got a bad vibe. If we did, we kept hiking.

I'd say something like, "Let's get going, we have to catch up with my husband."

Mom would want to 'pray over the meals.' That would've been ok, except she didn't want to listen to ME pray. My prayers didn't count. I was a Buddhist. So I insisted on a moment of silence in which we could each pray and not offend the other. She didn't think much of that idea, but sorta went along with it, begrudgingly.

I told her, "In the future we don't have to meet around meals. We could meet for a hike, meet for a movie, get coffee..."

Mom was all about food—that wouldn't change.

I told her, "I think if Jesus were alive today on Earth, he'd be a Buddhist. I think he'd be very angry with many of the so-called Christians."

We were slow hikers compared to the youngins. On our best day we did 12 miles, going to meet Brendon for a resupply. Generally, we hiked about 7 miles per day. We were happy with that. All we had to do all day was walk, eat, sleep, repeat. It felt very Zen like; putting me in the 'Zone.'

We enjoyed taking in the scenery as it went by, mile after mile. There was always something special: a flower, an animal, a special view, very difficult terrain, very pleasant and easy terrain, rocks, a nice stream, a waterfall, a road crossing, a special person... I would put some distance between us going up. Mom would catch up and pass me going down. We were a good team.

One evening, we heard thunder in the distance. It was nice weather that day, but the clouds were rolling in. We felt a few drops, but kept hiking.

A huge lightening bolt hit the ground in front of us, with a deafening "CRASHHhh," shaking the ground and blinding us. The rain came down in torrents, before we could find our pack covers and rain gear. The look on mom's face mirrored how I felt: scared. There was nowhere to run, nothing to do, we were soaked to the skin before we could react.

I approached hypothermia that evening, shivering violently for well over an hour in my tent which I placed inside the shelter (big no-no), wearing every clothing item I had, beginning with my silk long johns, long sleeved shirt, cashmere sweater, down jacket and rain/wind jacket; in sleeping bag. Many years later, I would think of the poor wild animals in the woods during violent storms. My watercress-green Patagonia rain/wind jacket became a trusted protector, and we became pros at getting on rain gear in a flash, stashing them at the top of our packs.

We ended up tenting half the time, sheltering half the time. I studied my official *A.T. Thru-Hikers' Companion* and *A.T. Data* books (both put out by the ATC-Appalachian Trail Conservancy) each night, planning for the next day. I bought A.T. Pocket Profile mini maps for each section. They were laminated, bonus. I tore the pages out of the guides for the section we were doing, to cut down on weight. Hell, I even broke the handles off of toothbrushes to save an ounce.

Physical limitations presented themselves regularly: earache one to two days, body aches almost every day, blisters occasionally, dehydration one to two days, shin splints one to three days, swollen ankles became chronic at the end, and poison ivy.

'Leaves of three, let it be'. I would if I could! Insect bites were kept at bay by the heavy duty DEET (90 something %). It was the only thing that seemed to work.

In the end, it was the swollen ankles and the pure pain in the balls of the feet that became intolerable. It helped for some time to duct tape them, giving them support and easing the pain. It was a hack learned from a fellow hiker. The knees were fine, although sometimes sore, thanks to the Cho-Pats. For mom, it was her shoulder. The weight/fit of her pack aggravated it, and although adjustments and movement helped, it bothered her for months after the 33 day hike.

We saw hikers throughout the days: anywhere from zero on one day, up to 71 (near a popular hiking/camping spot for the general public). On the average, we passed about a dozen hikers, usually going the other way—north. I calculated that there were about three women for every seven men on the trail, a little less than half.

At the shelters there were journals, usually a notebook with a pencil or pen in a ziplock. The backpackers would 'log in,' writing a blurb about their day, or leaving a message for someone coming behind them. The cartoons and drawings and poems were very entertaining after a whole day of hiking.

Pamarama made sure to sign each book at each shelter: Abingdon Gap, Double Springs, Iron Mountain, VanderVeeter, Laurel Fork, Apple House, Overmountain, Walnut Mountain, Cosby, TriCorner, Peck's Knob, Standing Indian, Plumorchard Gap, etc.

Everyone had trail names and used them when introducing themselves and to sign off in the journals. Pam became 'Pamarama' and mom became 'Granny (Long Legs).' Brendon and Saint were given the trail names, "just in case..."

The mother/daughter team got very experienced at peeing and taking a dump in the woods. There were plenty of trees and bushes to hide behind. We carried a roll of toilet paper, but also used leaves sometimes. We had a plastic orange backpacking hand shovel to bury the crap. It was a treat when there was a composting privy at a shelter. We were amused to find a privy that was open in front, with a killer view of the mountains, the 'best seat in the house,' indeed.

We bathed with wet wipes each night in the privacy of our solo backpacking tents. We were both happy we didn't have to worry about having our periods anymore.

At the end of the first week, we camped by beautiful Watauga Lake. At the Shook Branch Recreation Area there were young people swinging off a rope into the lake. I, Pamarama was tempted, but knew it would take forever to dry and the night would be cold up on the next mountain. Two nice trail angels came by (Mike and friend) and gifted cold Mountain Dew and treats.

Mom chuckled, "I hope they didn't notice my granny panties

drying in the sun."

We were near Braemer Castle Hostel, and we got a room for $15. We were able to wash our few clothes and eat microwave food—what a treat...And a soft bed. My Therm-a-Rest mattress, sleeping bag and Cocoon backpacking pillow were cozy, but a real bed was heaven. I called Brendon from a pay phone. He was visiting his folks up north.

One night we camped out in a beautiful rhododendron thicket. It was pitch-black that night after the sun went down.

I said, "Mom, it's so dark. I can't see my hand in front of my face. Can you?"

She said, "No, I can't either."

Another night while we were reclining in our backpacking tents, Granny/Mom whispered tersely,

"Pam! Look out your window."

There were 3 pairs of shining eyes stalking up the hill toward the tents.

I whispered loudly, "What are they? 'Possums?'"

Mom/Granny said, "Raccoons?"

I turned my Petzl headlamp towards them and they slunk away. The next night there was a lot of rustling outside the tents. We figured it might be deer or cows, as we had been near a cattle farm when we camped.

On our 12th day we ran across a sign for Mountain Harbor Hostel, two to three miles away. We got a room in a neat cabin above a barn, with horses and a nice creek. There were two nice younger guys, a young Asian guy Huang and Tony, who gave me a beer.

We got a $2 ride to the town of Roan Mountain and purchased moleskin, wash cream for poison, and Subway subs. We were in heaven eating our subs and washing them down with soda. $3 got our laundry done for us. Another call was made to Brendon with the approximate position for the first resupply.

We crossed over Hump Mountain which was a grassy bald (no

trees). African long-horned cattle were grazing topside.

Pamarama and Granny found Gray's Lily blooming near the Overmountain Shelter. It is a red nodding lily and rare. Overmountain Shelter is a three-storey barn. *Winter People* (Columbia Pictures) was filmed there. A local poet spoke with me and Granny and asked permission to mention us in his new book, but I lost his contact information.

ON THE 15TH DAY WE made it to Carver's Gap (5500') on Roan Mountain. It was very rainy, muddy and foggy. I begged a ride from a young couple back into town. I forgot and left my walking stick (the one mom had found at the Grand Canyon), in their SUV.

We met Brendon at Greasy Gap Friendly (not hostile/hostel—ha). It was our first resupply and we were happy to get rid of some not-so-useful, but heavy things we didn't need, including the trash we were carrying out. Ziggy doggy was along and the reunion was lovely. Brendon was happy to report, "I got a job and rented a house for us."

Mom got freaked out by a beautiful young man called Witch Doctor who was in the bunkhouse. He had done the entire A.T. twice. Mom couldn't get past the name. Laundry was done, two or three home-cooked meals were polished off, and the middle-aged couple who owned the place gave me a trekking pole that someone had left behind.

Mom and I decided to skip about 90 miles, between Roan Mountain and Hot Springs. In Hot Springs at Bluff Mountain Outfitters, I got some camp shoes I'd seen a few times on the trail. They were a new thang—light pink Crocs. They were perfect. They could easily be lashed to the pack, weighed a scant few ounces, were heaven on the feet after wearing the La Sportiva hiking boots all day. My feet had widened with all the walking and the boots were on the tight side. Going down mountains hurt the tips of my toes. The Smartwool socks

I bought helped.

We chilled on the porch of Elmer's Hostel, otherwise known as Sunnyland or Sunnybank Inn. It was like a museum of antiques. The owner was well known in the area and in the AT guide. We walked down the street to get a permit for the Smoky Mountains NP.

At the shelter on top of the next mountain, a nice guy gave us chocolate and water, as he was headed into Hot Springs for a resupply. We hiked over beautiful Max Patch Bald, very popular for day hikers in the area. The next day we saw some funky bright orange and HUGE mushrooms, shaped like fluted bowls.

A trail angel, Big Red's husband, handed out chilled Diet Coke the next day. Big Red had a head of red hair. She was the only single woman we saw on the trail that trip.

The Smokies was interesting, but became somewhat disappointing. It rained cats and dogs, and the trail became very muddy. In the park, horses are allowed on the trail, so the mud became mixed with horseshit. You were only allowed to camp right by the shelters, on pain of a ticket.

There WAS a nice fire tower (Mt. Cammerer fire tower), with an awesome view, even with some fog and wind. The balsam wooly adelgid had devastated portions of the woods, leaving the ghostly stumps of Frasier firs and conifers. It was a red/gray forest ghost town. EERIE.

On the 4th of July, the fireworks were the thunder/lightening storm that night. We shelter people laughed and joked about that, snuggly after having cooked our little meals on our little stoves, cozy in our sleeping bags.

There were 14 hikers in the next double decker shelter— Peck's Knob: nice older couple Sue & Tom, three brothers, young newlyweds, father with two young sons and Mike and friend (last seen at Watauga Lake). It turns out Mike had taken an interest in Mom/Granny and they had come looking for her. That gave mom renewed interest in the adventure!

THE 25TH DAY WAS PAM[arama] and Brendon's anniversary. We were going to meet up for the 2nd resupply. Tropical Storm Cindy did not make it easy for us. The trail became a creek, then a small rushing river, running off the mountain. We hiked with water over our boots, as there was nowhere else to go. We had to go slowly, as we didn't want to die in the flash flood. I had scary visions of mom breaking a leg or one of us drowning.

I went first, saying, "There's a rock moving here," or: "You'll sink in the mud there." We were freezing from hiking all day in the rain again, and with soaked feet.

We finally arrived at Newfound Gap on 421, about halfway through the Smokies. Brendon had been waiting some time. He bundled us into the car, turning up the heat at my bidding; not saying a word about our funky smell. He checked us into a hotel at Pigeon Forge, as Gatlinburg was full and expensive. He washed all our filthy clothes and came back with boxes of Bojangles chicken. I luxuriated in a hot bath for at least an hour. I never loved Brendon better than on that day, and had a moment of peace, when I thought maybe we could stay together forever.

Granny/Mom and Pamarama/I decided we were tired of the Smokies. Brendon & Ziggy drove us to Standing Indian Campground at Rock Gap. That was a little less than an hour by car from mom's house. We skipped the almost 100 miles between, midway in the Smokies to Standing Indian. The $14 campground site felt luxurious, with a real bathroom (we were now accustomed to trees and the composting johns that might be at the shelters) including showers, little store and pay phone.

Mom called Saint and he showed up with his daughter Caitlin and mom's friend Marie. Saint brought wood and built a lovely hot fire. We had only seen real fires a few times. Most serious backpackers used fuel canisters high up in the mountains. We were usually too beat to look for firewood. Also, it was often quite damp.

They brought a tasty watermelon and we roasted marshmallows—it was a real treat. Caitlin was NOT impressed with the tiny backpacking tents, saying, "Is that all?" She laughed when I mimed carrying a house on my back up a mountain.

We got a ride to the trailhead next morning by Mountain Man Dan. We saw the 2nd biggest poplar tree in the nation: Wasilik Poplar; 1 mile round trip, out of the way. A boy scout troupe of 30 (including three young priest guides) took up the entire next shelter, so we tented nearby. It rained that night and the tents were damp when we packed up.

Granny hoisted down the food sack most mornings while I, Pamarama slept in a bit. I hung them nightly with the lightweight nylon rope in the trees, to avoid the black bears. That morning she was sitting on a log when she opened the sack. A little mouse jumped out of the bag at her!

She jumped off the log and yelled, "AAaaaahhh!" I laughed until my face hurt, at the spectacle of Granny jumping and squealing, dropping the sack.

On day 30 we were hurrying to get to a shelter. I had heard on my wee transistor radio that Hurricane Charley was coming. We stayed at the shelter two nights while the rain and the trees blew sideways. We were cozy in our sleeping bags. An older guy and 21 year old Shifty were also in the shelter. Shifty had the book *Dharma Bums* by Jack Kerouac. I read the entire book, with relish.

After the second night, we made a run for it and arrived at the last NC shelter just before it started pouring again. The next morning we made a run for Plumorchard Gap. It was a beautifully crafted three-storey shelter.

A nice family of three from New Zealand and the girl's boyfriend from VA were there. The man was afraid of mice, shooing them off all night. That wouldn't have been so bad, except he kept his food near him instead of hanging it outside. I wanted to smack him the third time he woke us up, saying in a loud stage whisper to mom,

"If he'd put his food outside like everyone else, we wouldn't be having this problem."

On day 33, I cut the duct tape off of my feet and ankles. We were headed to mom's house. We stopped at Dick's Creek Gap and hitchhiked a ride in the back of a truck to the far end of the road that went to mom's house. We had enjoyed handing out some extra pack food to appreciative backpackers. Just a mile in, who should appear but Uncle Bryce, totally unplanned. He drove us the last couple of miles to mom's house.

WE HAD HIKED APPROXIMATELY 200 miles our first time out. Yay. All the family gathered for a picnic that weekend, about 30 in all. Clay's little fam, Saint's fam, and other assorted relatives. Mom and I looked good, sporting new haircuts and having gotten body wraps. Mom let me dye her hair for the first (and last) time. We had each lost about 20 pounds and would keep it off the next decade plus. My feet had grown. The pads were pretty much gone, and I now wore a size 7.

Our self-confidence had also grown. For mom, it was the beginning of a real independence. She had always been dependent on men: first her dad and then her husband. She would always put more stock into what men would say/preach, but she began to question more. She began to stand up for herself and to make decisions that sometimes went against the grain, which Saint did not appreciate.

I/Pam/Pamarama would never look at the mountains the same way. I had conquered them. Of course, they had allowed it or we could've died in so many ways...They became familiar friends.

Granny and Pamarama would go on another backpacking trip of about two weeks, completing another 85 miles or so, a few years later. We began at the southernmost blaze on the A.T., at Springer

Mountain. Saint and his daughter Caitlin shouldered our backpacks over a mile, to get to the starting point. They expressed appreciation for the effort it took.

We would arrive at Gooch Mountain Shelter and find all women there—a first. There were two close friends and another mother/daughter team, much younger. There was a wonderful camaraderie and one of the women took photos and sent them to us later.

The adventures kept coming. A couple of wild pigs ran across the trail in front of me. I walked right over a snake on the trail. We camped on one of the balds. It was a lovely day, with an almost 360 degree view. That night, the wind picked up. It almost picked up our little tents and blew them over the mountain! The only thing holding them to the ground, was the weight of our bodies and backpacks, as the tents blew sideways right over our faces. I'm pretty sure we were both saying our individual prayers on that windy night, but the wind was so loud you could hardly think. Needless to say, we didn't get much sleep that night.

Blood Mountain Shelter was super steep and had an old stone shelter. You could just feel the energy of the Native Americans battling. Although my DNA never showed any Native North American ancestors, Our DNA would inform us that mom and I were part Native South American, from the Andes Mountain region.

On July 4th, 2010, Pamarama and Granny found themselves once again on the A.T. We passed over the road that goes to Helen, GA. We debated going to Helen to celebrate the 4th, but decided to continue on. We camped out beside a Native American princess' burial mound.

I placed a couple of blooms on the mound to honor her. That night, instead of lightning and thunder fireworks, we were snug in our bags when we heard a blood curdling scream. I had heard that sound one time before, on Grandma Fawn and Grandpa Chester's porch.

Mom and I whispered loudly, "What was that?"

I guessed, "Bobcat?"

Mom said, "'Painter?'"

It sounded like a woman screaming. Although the scream of large wild cat is freaky-scary, I felt protected and honored. Besides, our food was up in the trees and we had our large bear spray canisters beside us in our tents.

That trip filled in one of the three gaps we had left from Damascus, VA to Springer Mountain, GA. The other two gaps would be filled in with a boyfriend, two grandkids and finally solo. I would complete my 500 miles, almost a quarter of the A.T. I did all of Georgia, North Carolina, Tennessee and then some.

I was cradled in the bosom of the mountains. I walked up and down, up and down her. We created an intimate relationship together.

AFTER THAT MAJOR FEAT, the first hospice job I checked on hired me and I was able to get free licensing/supervision hours at my new job. It took two years of intensive work to complete my license requirements. I now had more letters after my name: MSW, LCSW (Masters of Social Work, Licensed Clinical Social Worker), and I was very marketable.

In the meantime, Brendon and I bought a house. It was during a small window after working for a year in our "new" state and before Brendon began college. I hesitated, knowing I would be making most of the payments and also knowing in my heart that this marriage would most likely fail. However, we were still in love and still trying to improve ourselves and our relationship.

It worked for about seven years total. We were very busy, working and studying and playing with Ziggy. Every night when Brendon came home from the restaurant where he was a chef, he'd bring something special to eat. I'd have a glass or two (at least three for him) of port, while watching HBO.

We had family over and he cooked large holiday meals while I cleaned, decorated and hosted. However, our sex life dwindled and I grew unhappy. To Brendon's credit, he never relapsed again while we were together.

I began taking Bikram Hot Yoga classes, which I loved. I also began going to a Tibetan style Buddhist center: FPMT — Foundation for the Preservation of the Mahayana Tradition. It was linked to HH Dalai Lama. I had gone to SGI in N. Carolina for a while after moving, but felt that something was missing for me.

I took refuge formally: in Buddha, dharma and sangha, the Three Jewels. I was given a Buddhist name—Gyalten Chodoen, by the Refuge Master—Ven. Kyabje Choden Rinpoche. I began to study dharma and to learn the names of the various buddhas. It took some getting used to: being in a room with Buddhist statues and paraphernalia. I realized what had been missing: tantra, to balance the sutra.

Brendon and I attended Buddhist teachings together at times. He did it for me. He claimed to like it, but had a bit of a contemptuous air and became impatient. I assured him it would be better if he didn't go, if he really wasn't feeling it.

———————◉———————

HE SEEMED TO BE DRINKING more. His hidden cigarette smoking resurfaced when he started another fire. He had been smoking in SoCal, pretending to take the garbage out each evening. I smelled smoke and looked out the window, seeing smoke down by the garage. I freaked out, having lived through one of the first major fires in SoCal. Brendon had been out of town and hadn't experienced the soupy, ashy, pea-green air that shut down the big city for days.

He denied smoking, but I found cigarettes hidden in his truck. This time he'd dropped his ashes into a brush pile. When I looked outside, the brush pile was burning very high and hot, in danger of catching everything on fire. There was no one in sight. He admitted it this time, but was angry. His resentment seemed to build and it effected our relationship. It got to the point we were having sex maybe every other month. I decided I was done. I couldn't trust him. We weren't close anymore and he wasn't trying. I gave up.

I turned the house over to him legally. He quickly got a woman pregnant and told me,   .

"If you want to just give me your diamond ring, we can call it even."

I retorted, "I've EARNED that ring. I'll give you a couple thousand to get started." I figured he was planning to give the ring to his new lover.

We divided up the furniture and he got the bigass tv. We kept our own vehicles. Ziggy stayed with me initially, but my work hours were hurting her. With tears rolling down my cheeks, I turned our beloved poochie-poo over to her dad. He and his new lover had more time for a dog. I would always wonder what happened to Ziggy and missed her dreadfully.

I realized I was no longer in love with Brendon, but wished him well. The most lovely thing from that 4th marriage was all the gourmet meals cooked for me by my personal loving chef. I forgave all and the resentments fell away.

In retrospect, I could see how the fundamentalism mixed with the sexual abuse had taken its toll on my relationships over the years. I pondered my relationship karma. I was grateful that I had learned not to settle and had the strength to move on when I needed to. It was much more than just *The Seven-Year Itch:* I realized that without trust and communication, relationships are doomed. I thought sometimes—*maybe I should become a Buddhist nun.*

8. The Love of My Life

An old crush resurfaced on a new social media website online: Facebook. He was my beloved and beautiful band director from high school, Mr. F. When I changed my relationship status on FB, the light banter between us took on a more romantic nature, with sexual undertones. I began to call him by his first name, Miguel.

Within a couple of weeks, we had planned a weekend date. We would meet halfway between our homes, about three hours away by car. A few days before our 'lost weekend,' he dropped a bombshell in an email:

'I have to tell you something that may change your mind about meeting me. I found out a short time ago that I have an aggressive cancer. Cancer that could kill me or take away my ability to have an erection. I understand if you might want to wait until after my scheduled surgery, to meet.'

I was floored. I had ALWAYS loved him. Everyone loved him. I thought about it overnight.

I wrote him back:

"I have always had a big crush on you. I've always wanted to be close to you. I want to go ahead, while we know we have a little time and see what happens."

I knew in my heart that I wanted to be with him no matter for how long or in what form. I wanted to be there for him.

We met at a restaurant bar. I arrived first and was sipping on a cocktail when he arrived. He was 15 years older, unlike several of my past relationships, in which *I* was several years to a decade older.

He tried to use that information later, saying, "You're a 'cougar.'"

I said, "Yes, I've been a 'cougar,' but (and it's a big butt, we would joke) I'm not *your* cougar, so you don't get to call me that."

He liked that I was younger, like many men of means who would take younger and younger lovers as time went on. He was also a bit embarrassed.

Mom said, "He looks his age."

He acted youthfully and was clearly the same person. He had those same beautiful blue eyes, although not quite as bright. His longish brown hair was now gray. He was a few inches taller than me and he still had a beard and mustache. His clothes were a bit dated and he was set in his ways, but I had decided before meeting him that it did not matter to me how he looked. His eyes went over my body and I gave him a little kiss as he was gazing into my eyes with a knowing look.

He said, "I have some wine and cheese in the room—do you want to talk there?"

It was a little awkward that first weekend. We did fun things: a museum, walking around, a zoo. He would produce a nice bottle of wine each evening we were together. Even when I gave up pork, beef and alcohol a few years later, he would give me a bottle to denature so we could enjoy a drink together.

We DID become intimate, connecting on all levels, not knowing if that might be our only chance. The next week he had his surgery and I couldn't see him.

As we were out taking a little walk, he gazed into my eyes and we kissed. He held me close to him and said very softly into my ear, "I love you." I was so happy, but a bit surprised that he would say that on our first weekend together.

He recovered in his sister's city. His therapy included taking a little blue pill and masturbation. His surgery had not taken away his ability to have an erection and he had to keep the blood flowing. We were so relieved he had had laparoscopic surgery, rather than the more common—radical surgery.

We began to make plans to see each other again and I became

his sex therapist, helping him rehabilitate after surgery. Many do not realize that after the prostate gland is removed, a man does not ejaculate semen. During the next several years we would happily have sex twice a day when we were together. It was regular, missionary position sex, but it gave us joy and comfort.

I had made plans to go to Hawaii before I began dating Miguel. Turns out he owned a pink house with a heart-shaped pool and an ocean view: in Hawaii.

Miguel said, "It'll be our 'honeymoon,' and happy 50th birthday." I thanked him for giving me such a wonderful gift and felt grateful.

———◦———

DINNER ON THE LANAI was an unhurried and very pleasant affair, beginning with the blowing of the conch at sunset, with toasts and ending with much conversation. The cute geckos had full run of the lanai and the whole house. It was fun watching them chase each other through the shadows. The whole vibe of Hawaii was different: slower, more chill. Drivers were more patient and polite. We went to so many of Miguel's favorite spots.

We hiked to green sand beach (Mahana Beach)—a very isolated spot down a cliff-like embankment. It had actual green-tinted sand from olivine sand, eroded out of the enclosing volcanic cone. It was near South Point, the southernmost point of Hawaii and also of the USA. Miguel dived with others over the cliff into the Pacific.

I counted 17 sea turtles at one beach, and we kayaked out to Captain Cook on Kealakekua Bay. We snorkeled, enjoying the colorful tropical fish and coral, which was spectacular. I held on to him for dear life.

He often teased me, saying, "You had a 'death grip' on me, but I'm proud of you for having the courage to go out, being a weak swimmer."

I was happy that he seemed to want to show me off, introducing me to his friends, a few who came to stay at Pink House while we were there. I wondered what they thought about the moans and groans coming out of our open bedroom window each day.

Later I would understand that he enjoyed having an entourage around him. He enjoyed having friends with, many of whom were well-positioned like him. Others were "hangers on" who benefitted much more than they gave. He enjoyed being 'Top Dog' and would often drop subtle hints (especially to women) about the vehicles and properties he owned, or the exotic trips he took.

I was initially turned off by his wealth. I had been taught as a child: 'It's easier for a camel to go through the eye of a needle than it is for a rich man to enter into the gates of heaven.'

I told him, "You may be out of my league." He laughed. I wondered how a teacher could have done so well materially. He and his ex-wife had dabbled in real estate and turns out they were really good at it.

Unfortunately, she had cheated on him with a mutual acquaintance for a couple of years at the end of their marriage, and finally left him. I vowed to myself to never give him a reason to doubt me.

Miguel, however, was flirty at times. Men had always liked him and women competed for his attention. He knew how to use that to his advantage. Mom even noticed when he flirted with her sister, Aunt Sue. I called him out for his inappropriate remarks and/or looks a few times during our years together, saying with exasperation,

"You're always on the make." He laughed.

He claimed to be a Christian, choosing his churches based on their choirs and music programs and some of his real friends that attended. He enjoyed the friendships of those solid church types, but gloried in persuading them to be "sinful," encouraging several Southern Baptists to start drinking and dancing. He was Republican, but that seemed to be related to the $$$ and not to the social issues so much.

He didn't care that I was a Buddhist. He even went with me to a couple of Buddhist teachings after I moved closer to him and mom. I went with him a couple of times to his Baptist church, when he was playing a piano solo, or there was some special holiday music program.

He was proud of me and my accomplishments. He valued education and travel. He also had a Master's degree and had traveled the world. He didn't seem to care that I had been married and divorced several times. He understood there were 'deal breakers.'

We had a lot in common, and had fun talking like hillbillies and making silly jokes with each other. He told me my accent reminded him of his mother's. We both loved the South and southerners, but could move between the worlds with ease.

I was especially happy to have Miguel back in my life after dad died. He knew my family because we had all been in the high school band. I had lost an important ally in dad. With Miguel, I once again had a powerful ally; not just in the family, but in the larger community. He believed in me. He appreciated my mind. He understood my worth.

I had a lovely dream about Miguel, in which he had his arm around me, protectively. I could see some enemies behind us, but he was shielding me. I had a wonderful feeling of security, like no one could harm me while I was with him.

———◆———

HE HAD GONE OUT ON dates with a couple of former students, but nothing seriously. He had actually gone out with cousin Bobbie a couple of times, years before. He said they had kissed, she denied that. He had said he couldn't get past the fact that she hadn't grown-up at all since high school, acting like a silly girl. She said she couldn't get past the fact that he was our old teacher.

I walked up to Great Aunt Ruby's, above mom's house. Bobbie was getting paid to take care of our great aunt and had a couple of other family members living there with her.

I asked Bobbie directly, "Do you still have any interest in Mr. F? I know you got together with him a couple of times a few years ago."

Bobbie said, "No. I'm happy for you, you deserve him."

A few months later a mutual cousin would confirm that Bobbie had stolen tens of thousands of dollars from Great Aunt Ruby. She had gotten access to her bank account and drained the money out.

I would never feel close to her again. She clearly hadn't learned any longterm lessons after her arrest some years before. The deaths of my once close, loving relationships with Bobbie and Saint hurt greatly.

Miguel and I began taking turns every weekend, driving three hours one way, to visit each other. The visits always seemed too short. I struggled at times, working all week and then being gone every other weekend.

Although he had expressed his love that first weekend; in reality, I always loved Miguel more than he loved me. Maybe he only ever truly loved himself. We were both Pisces with complex personality, quirky sense of humor and keen intellect.

Those days were 'mahhvelous.' We went places and did things and enjoyed just being together. My family was very surprised, but pleased after a short time to have Miguel joining in family meals and events. He flattered mom and we often went out as a threesome.

I would take him to extended family events, sharing him with the cousins who had also been in band. They always expressed more interest in me when he was around.

———◉———

EARLY ON, I ASKED HIM: "Are we dating exclusively?"

He hemmed and hawed and suggested, "Maybe that is not necessary?"

I said, "Well I guess I'll just keep playing the field until I get what I want, then." With that, he agreed that we would be exclusive.

I questioned his fidelity a couple of times throughout our relationship. He always said, "No. I haven't been with anyone else."

I never had a reason not to believe him, although I found out from someone very close to him that he had cheated on his last girlfriend for several years when she had thought *they* were exclusive. Miguel had to be nailed down, or he would 'beat the devil around the bush' indefinitely and do what he wanted, undercover.

He told me solemnly, "You will leave me for a younger man someday."

I looked into his eyes and said earnestly, "Not if you treat me right." I knew in my heart I would stay with him forever and lovingly care for him in his last months and years, if needed.

Three or four times per year he would go out of town to visit his other properties and friends. He had places in Alaska and Ecuador, in addition to Hawaii and the southern mountains. He would go away for several weeks, enjoying his retirement and friends while I worked my butt off. It *did* give me a chance to relax and not have to drive every other weekend during the only time I had free.

A couple times per year he would invite me to come join him and would often pay for half my plane ticket. He loaned me his old iPhone and I gave him $50 for his old GPS. Over the years he gifted me with several devices: a Kindle, Kindle Fire and an iPad mini.

I told him, "If you want to give me something, give it to me without any strings or expectations, just because. I don't plan to be a kept woman who owes you."

We often shared books and music. He had a lovely grand piano and would sing me romantic songs, such as "An Affair to Remember" (Vic Damone). It became *our* song.

During those first years, we had few real disagreements. There was one early incident that gave me pause. Miguel let slip that he had an STD (sexually transmitted disease). We had talked about STDs before we had met up. He had said he wasn't aware of having anything. He had lied, talking like it wasn't a big deal, minimizing it, saying he was always careful not to have sex if/when he had a breakout.

I liked to have blown a gasket. I let him have it, full blast. I insisted on getting tests done immediately. Sure enough, I now had the same kind of STD he did. I was very unhappy and considered strongly whether I should stay with him or not.

He said, "Now you hate me," hanging his head.

I decided I was already infected, I could get treated. I loved him, I stayed and forgave.

I asked him, "Are you *SURE* you don't have other secrets you're keeping from me? Anything *ELSE* I need to know? *NOW* is your chance to tell me. You know I can't stay with a liar."

He assured me, "There is nothing else."

My life was full and I was happy overall, after I got over the STD debacle. I was working on forgiveness and I knew I had plenty of imperfections.

———————◉———————

ON THE CAREER FRONT, I had meaningful work that I loved and was good at. I really liked the new hospice team.

I learned even more about human nature, seeing folks at the end of their lives. Mostly, they died as they lived. If they always had drama around them, they often died in a dramatic way, with families fighting and drugging until the end. Others died very calmly and positively with little pain or drama. They died joyfully, fearfully, angrily and lovingly.

Over the years, Christians would sometimes ask me, "Do Christians usually die easier?"

I had to tell them truthfully, "No. I've experienced atheists and agnostics and folks with other religions/faiths die just as well or better."

Indeed, it often seemed to me that the Christians worried too much about going to hell and that made them fearful. Some would question god when THEY got sick. They expected no less than a miracle healing. A worried person, or an angry person, or a fearful person, or a person in a lot of pain often died a less peaceful death.

As a social worker, I would help them live until they died by engaging them in life review, providing counseling related to anticipatory grief and being sure they had the resources (physical, mental & emotional) that they needed.

I became comfortable with death and its processes. I could provide therapeutic presence to a patient who was comatose and even perhaps with other issues present, such as gangrene. The rotten stench would fade with revery and silent prayers for the dying.

The patients would usually accept they were dying at some point, but the families would sometimes be in denial until the end. I never understood when a 90 something year old would say something like: 'If only I could eat (or sleep or walk) again, I could get better.'

I wanted to say, "Wake-up! You're dying! Everyone dies. Prepare thyself," but I would, of course, have to be the diplomatic social worker. I would be with them at whatever emotional/spiritual/mental level they were at, and work from there.

For the often charismatic, evangelical Christian folk that were expecting to be healed; I would allow that,

"Certainly that is possible. However, you might want to consider that your healing might take place in (Christian) Heaven."

Death became my touchstone, guiding my thoughts and actions and meditations going forward. I worked hard at normalizing death for others, breaking with taboos firmly put in place over the last decades.

———⊙———

I BEGAN GOING TO A Vajrayana (Tibetan style) Buddhist center nearby. I was fortunate to find an intimate center with a couple dozen practitioners. I received a lot of one on one attention from a wonderful practitioner who became a Buddhist nun.

I began to learn so much more. It might have been timing, or it might have been the group. I would later realize that the teachings of the Guru, Venerable Geshla Kelsang Gyatso Rinpoche, were very clear and focused. He wrote many dharma books, translating from Tibetan to English. He had at least one important teacher that he shared in common with the Dalai Lama, and they had much the same lineage.

They had both had to escape over the Himalayan Mountains at the time of the Chinese invasion. They shared most of the same beliefs, but at some point the Dalai Lama turned his back on one of the Dharma Protectors; making the protector out to be a demon, and therefore making Geshla's sangha group (followers/students) out to be malevolent.

Anyone can look up the particulars of the controversy. The thing was, while the Dalai Lama was the head of one group of Buddhists, similar to the Christian Catholic Pope, there were many other groups and they were supposed to all be autonomous. Just as the Pope doesn't speak for all Christians, the Dalai Lama doesn't speak for all Buddhists.

Most westerners don't understand this and it has caused much negativity, needlessly. The Buddhist Americans I spoke with over the years didn't seem to have any animosity towards Geshla Kelsang Gyatso. They also didn't seem to question the status quo with the Dalai Lama. Many of Geshla's followers were ostracized. In Tibet and even in India, they were sometimes in danger of physical harm.

To my ex-Protestant mind, the Tibetan (Vajrayana) Buddhists were the latest, most progressive, the **esoteric** bunch of the lot. They could be equated with the Gnostic Christians or the Jewish Kabbalist. Mom would 'throw off' on the "New Wave" teachings, and I would tell her the teachings were from ancient thought before Christianity, not a new age.

I often thought about a fundamentalist FB friend who had called me out publicly on going to a women's protest and carrying signs as a Liberal. I was in good company with the MILLIONS of women who protested in the USA and worldwide on Jan. 21, 2017, just before I went on pilgrimage. I reminded her that as a Protestant, the word "protest" was their root word. She had to concede.

I had one last dream about dad. I described it to mom:
I'm walking through a temple with Buddhist robes on

*(mom had met two of my Buddhist nun friends and saw
them in their gold and burgundy robes). I have a smile
and I'm happy. I'm getting ready to teach dharma. I
position myself on the 'throne,' smoothing my robe
around me. I look out into the audience with a smile. Dad
is in the audience! He looks serious; he's taking the
teaching seriously. HE HAS ON ROBES!*

I got choked up as I always did when I remembered my most
special 'Dad Dream.' The dream said to me that dad approved of my
spirituality and religion. He was able to actually *learn something* from
his daughter. He was putting himself below her; his robes were a
novice's robes. I also knew at that point that I had most likely been a
Buddhist nun in a past life.

Mom said, "Well I don't think your dad is a Buddhist. I don't think
you should tell people that."

I replied, "Mom, it's a dream. MY dream. I can interpret it the way
it feels/seems to me."

She just raised her eyebrows and let it go.

To me, it was a practical matter. I was very happy to find a heart
guru who could lay out the ancient teachings in such an easy to
understand manner. The ways of practice too, were becoming easier to
understand. I was able to separate the teachings from the traditional
Tibetan culture, which made me appreciate both more. I realized that
it was the Tantra that I had been missing and the fuller teachings of the
Sutras.

Many Americans hear "tantra," and immediately think of sex. It
is SO much more complex and intricate than that. The definition,
according to Geshla's book: *The New Meditation Handbook* (by Geshe
Kelsang Gyatso) says:

*Synonymous with Secret Mantra, Tantric teachings are
distinguished from Sutra teachings in that they reveal*

methods for training the mind by bringing the future
result, or Buddhahood, into the present path. Tantric
practitioners overcome ordinary appearances and
conceptions by visualizing their body, environment,
enjoyments, and deeds as those of a Buddha. Tantra is the
supreme path to full enlightenment. Tantric practices are
to be done in private and only by those who have received
a Tantric empowerment.

I still chanted or sang verses/sutras during *sadhanas* or *pujas*, but began meditating in silence more. It was not the meditation of nothingness, but on Lamrim, the stages of the path to enlightenment. It was all coming together for me and I realized:

Enlightenment is actually possible in this very life.

Vajrayana or Tantric Buddhism is the quick path, the lightning bolt path to this enlightenment. And becoming a Bodhisattva on that path would definitely insure the result. Such a person would reach nirvana but would delay themselves, for the fulfillment of all sentient beings to also become enlightened.

I knew intuitively, as a "helping professional" that helping anyone on this earth is limited. One can advocate for and assist others, but it never seems to be enough. The problems of the world are endless: deep and wide and countless. Maybe that is why there are so many well educated Buddhists who are also in the Helping Professions.

I realized the only way I can really help anyone is to pray for and advocate for their enlightenment, but first I must become enlightened myself. As in an airplane, I would put my own oxygen on first, so I could assist others. I would not do that by proselytizing, but would meet people where they were.

I felt solid, like the parts of my life were congruent: social work, hospice, meditation, buddhism, yoga, psychology...

THE MONTHS AND YEARS went by. I visited Miguel's places in Hawaii and Ecuador several times. We hiked behind a waterfall in Banos, and kissed, congratulating ourselves on crawling on our bellies at one point to get behind the waterfall.

On the way, we were able to view Cotopaxi—one of the highest active volcanoes in the world. It was snow covered at the peak. We took the TeleferiQo Cruz Loma gondola lift about 3,000' up a mountain in Quito and I took a donkey up into the Andes another mile plus. Quito is already over 10,000'. I got up to almost 14,000'.

We took a speed boat out to Isla de la Plata: Island of Silver, 'Poor man's Galapagos.'

I was so excited walking up to and seeing the Blue Footed Boobie up close: "Wow—they actually DO have blue feet." They were nesting on the ground and didn't get very excited about us being there.

Miguel pointed, "Look!" There was a giant albatross. He took the opportunity next, to snorkel with the sea turtles.

We took a wonderful Alaskan ferry boat cruise, changing ferries a couple of times, all the way to Pelican. I bought a beautiful recycled, seal-fur teddy bear there, which one of the Grands inherited and lost at some point.

We met the entourage of extended family and friends there and I had a beer (on my own dime) with Miguel's brother in law and nephew, at the famous Rosie's Bar & Grill. Miguel refused, on principle, to ever drink before 5:00 p.m.

I flew back to work while Miguel stayed for his annual fishing trip. At the end of the cruise, we saw a pod of whales perform a feeding dance. There was about 10 of them, in a circle, and they did appear to actually be doing a synchronized dance. I was entranced.

I had gotten close to a whale once in San Diego. The whale cruise would find them by sonar. The whale had breached and blew through its hole. This was that, on steroids, much as everything in Alaska was.

I TRAVELED SOME ON my own, as well. I went to Portugal for a retreat: NKT-IKBU International Fall Festival, 2013. I was ecstatic to receive teachings in person by Geshla. He conferred the empowerment of Prajnaparamita and taught the *Uncommon Yoga of Inconceivability* (translated by Geshe Kelsang Gyatso). My mind was blown. I had much to ponder that would take the rest of this life. I studied *The New Heart of Wisdom* (by Geshe Kelsang Gyatso) to get started.

I took a few days on that trip to sightsee, from Cascais to Lisboa (Lisbon). The cliff faces of Boca do Inferno were nearby the retreat site at the Hipodromo. I luxuriated in the sea air, hiking along the beach.

I took the yellow tram to the 7 hills, walked under the Arches of Arco da Victoria and the Rua Augusta (at the main port area). I saw other famous and ancient sites: the 18th century Basilica Da Estrela, National Monument, Palace of Pena, Moorish Castle, Jeronimos Monastery from famous tram #28, Torre de Belem Tower (16th century UNESCO site), Lisbon Cathedral (12th century)...

The trams came very close to house walls and trees, they looked like they were going to collide while you were riding along with the window down. A sign said something like: *Keep your hands and head in to prevent injury or death.*

The people and food were sensational. My favorite restaurant was the Jardim dos Frangos, where I relished the grilled chicken with piri piri sauce, with half a bottle of Mateus. For dessert I had the famous Ginjinha (cherry liquor) on the street. Chargrilled sardines, big fat ones, were also a treat and very popular. They were sold in fancy, decorated tins.

I enjoyed hanging out with other retreatants and talking with the Portuguese people on the narrow cobblestone streets. More than a dozen Buddhist friends (sangha) rented a villa together, which was hectic.

I was last to arrive, and all the good beds were taken. I decided to pull the blow-up mattress behind the sofa in a nook of the house. It turned out to be a good idea. I had more privacy than most and the powder room was nearby.

Before the retreat I would give up beef and pork and after I would give up alcohol (98%). I had had enough of each, time to set them aside for the sake of enlightenment, for all sentient beings. I would not spit out food if I accidentally took in beef or pork, but would never ask for it or order it again. I *did* allow for a celebratory drink on a special occasion, about twice per year. It was not a chore to let go more harmful foods and I did not crave them nor regret my decision.

I would definitely go back to Portugal, given the chance. Miguel and I had talked about going together to hike the Camino de Santiago from Porto. That would have been so cool. However, I thought better of it when the reason for going to Portugal became more about the hike than the special retreat I had longed for. Besides, I didn't have enough vacation time to do both properly.

The following year I traveled to Hong Kong for the Asian Festival retreat on Lantau Island. I received my Highest Yoga Tantra empowerment/initiation of Vajrayogini and Heruka from Genla Khyenrab. It was very involved with intricate meditations and visualizations. It would take me several years to take it all in and begin to understand the enormity of it all.

Before and after the retreat I did a bit of touring, taking a large speedboat to Macau. There was a nice Buddhist temple there—Na Tcha Temple. There were a lot of casinos, similar to Las Vegas, some with the same names.

I had a large meal, sampling some of the local delicacies: 1000 year old egg, congee and chrysanthemum tea at Noodle and Dim Sum Kitchen. When I bit into the egg, it had a pungent, ammonia-like smell. It looked black, but gelatinous. It tasted like an egg, but with a bitter bite to it.

I took the wonderful and exciting Ngong Ping 360 gondola lift which went on forever, over the Tung Chung Bay. It ended up at the

Big Buddha statue that sat in meditation, protecting and blessing Hong Kong.

Another day I went with a sangha friend who had also come for the retreat, to The Grand Hall of Ten Thousand Buddhas in Sha Tin area. Indeed, there were thousands of Buddha statues going all the way up both sides of a big hill, small mountain. They were all different.

The Victoria Peak tram took me to the highest viewing terrace, 1300' above sea level. The Kowloon ferry took me to the Avenue of Stars (similar to Hollywood's Walk of Fame) and promenade, where I viewed a junk with a red sail in Victoria Harbor. Bruce Lee and Jackie Chan are the stars I remember. On the way back, I witnessed the nightly laser light show on the water.

I stayed at a hostel in Causeway Bay and used my Octopus Card to take the various buses (N11, E11) back and forth, and the subway. I enjoyed being around a lot of people, but also having a lot of privacy. I was good at being largely incognito in a crowd.

I ate at a couple of Michelin Star restaurants. My favorite restaurant was Lin Heung Tea House where mostly locals ate traditional dim sum. I had to share a table, it was so packed. I pointed at what I wanted from off the carts that rolled by.

On the way back to Causeway Bay, I walked past the protestors: part of the 'yellow umbrella protest,' towards the end. The protestors were literally camped out with tents on the tram line. Different speakers would speak from a microphone.

A youngish woman asked me, "Hold please."

I said, "Sure."

I held a protest sign while she taped it up on a post. I felt like I had helped a bit with their protest for democracy, never suspecting our own democracy in the good ole US of A, would also be in jeopardy in a few years. I felt the pain deeply when Hong Kong got swallowed by China, soon after.

I was so glad I had made it to Hong Kong before the Chinese were victorious. I wished I could have gone to Tibet before the Chinese ruined *it*, however I was not yet born. I refused to go to Tibet and give the Chinese government the satisfaction. I knew I would have been resentful with watchful Chinese looking over my shoulder, knowing how they had desecrated everything I would have come to see.

———◦———

I TOOK MY OLDEST TWO grands on a trip to SoCal, staying with brother Nate. I took them to all my old haunts. They had never flown on an airplane before. They got to ride the trains and trolley. They went to the beach and to the desert. They stood with Grandma Pam, or Pamaw, looking into Tijuana, but couldn't go into Mexico because they didn't have passports. We had fun with Uncle Nate and Aunt Selena (my old friend from hospice who had married Nate).

On a very different trip, Clay dropped me and the grands off on the side of an isolated road and we backpacked on the A.T. for three days and nights; ending up crossing the river into Hot Springs.

I was impressed that they kept up with my fast hiking and they seemed to enjoy the adventure. We stayed at a shelter one night, tented a night, and then stayed at the same victorian style hostel (Elmer's Hostel) I had stayed at with mom; on my first A.T. adventure, approaching from the opposite direction.

Our threesome enjoyed soaking in a hot tub, fed by the hot mineral springs. We laughed and talked. I was so happy to be with them. Their mother did not appreciated me being a Buddhist. She was similar to mom (and they remain friends to this day) in her beliefs and she had a lot of influence over Clay during their early years. I had to bite my tongue a few times when their mother started bitching about Clay in front of everyone. I wanted to tell her off. She seemed to think she could get me on her side. *Dream. On.* I was relieved when they divorced, except it was difficult for the kids. Divorce is never easy on the kids.

WEEKENDS WERE SET ASIDE for Miguel and family. They were spent lovemaking, drinking wine, going to a cheap restaurant and to mom's. Laundry was done there, free. Little outings were frequent: to hike, to see a local concert, to go boating on the lake.

Miguel owned a nice speed boat and had access to a big pontoon boat for bigger groups. He would take out my family and our friends. The 4th of July was special. We speeded over to the fireworks and watched from the boat, along with other boaters. We often went out on the lake for the sunset, brie and red wine in tow. Before he got his boat, we would go out on the jet ski. I draped my arms around him and never wanted to let go.

We went to a church sale and the old woman at the cash box asked me,

"Doesn't your husband give you a big enough allowance?"

She assumed that a younger woman with an older man didn't work or have any money of her own and had to beg her husband to buy her a few used trinkets.

I began bitching, out in the car: "That old bat."

Miguel laughed at my discomfort. He knew I could and did take care of myself. Indeed, he was the only partner I'd ever had in this life that made more money than I did. He was my only equal in education, and comparable in travel for our ages.

That reminded me of a similar incident in Ecuador. We had gone to a party of ex-pats. An older (but not much older) woman who had never spoken to me before, asked me derisively,

"How long have you known Miguel?"

You could have seen her mouth hit the floor when I replied, "Oh, 40 years."

I wondered, *did she think that Miguel had picked me up off the street that day or last week?* Most people thought I was at least a decade younger than I was, which would have made me a quarter of a century younger than Miguel.

She said, "OH, that's good...." She didn't speak another word to me that night.

————————◆————————

I LONGED TO LIVE CLOSER to Miguel and to mom. After working for several years at that hospice, I gave notice and took a trip across country with Miguel. After, I quickly found another hospice job near him & mom; closer to Clay, his new wife, and the (now four) Grands.

We took Miguel's BMW, driving to Dallas, TX. While there, we went to the delightful Perot Museum and to the spooky 6th Floor Museum (where JFK's assassin shot him down).

I went out to lunch with ex-husband #3. We met him in the lobby, Miguel stayed behind. Shane had called mom after the court-ordered three years. I finally called him back after much thought. He apologized profusely many times. We talked occasionally after that. He had married an American Muslim woman who had two daughters. They had moved to Texas and would soon have three children of their own. They made a lot of money together and had a big house, reportedly.

He had long hair and still looked attractive. He took me to an expensive restaurant.

He said, "I'm so sorry I wouldn't eat with you in Pakistan because I thought it was too expensive. I thank my god you did not send me back to Pakistan."

I was happy to see him and could easily forgive him now. He had learned a lot living in America and regretted his mistakes.

We drove on to San Diego and put Miguel's BMW on a container ship headed to Hawaii. We spent a few days with Nate and his wife Selena, going to Balboa Park and the Midway Museum in San Diego Bay.

We got on a plane and flew to Oahu. We spent a few days in

Honolulu, going to see the local sights. The Pearl Harbor site was haunting. You could see the sunken ship below the monument/museum. You had to take a boat out to it. The most touching part to me, was reading the plaque in the far room where rows of cremation vases sat. Some of the dead had remained in the sunken ship. Some of their mates who had lived, opted to be cremated and placed near their sunken mates for eternity, after their own deaths.

Bishop Museum was very entertaining and educational. I felt bad for the native Hawaiians who had lost so much to those who had replaced them. It was named after Charles Reed Bishop who had married the last descendant of the royal Kamehameha family: Princess Bernice Pauahi.

Then it was on to Big Island and pink house for a month. We did a lot in that month. We visited several waterfalls (Akaka, Rainbow, etc.), went to the eastern/wet part of the island and stayed in Hilo a few days. We tried to go to where the lava was flowing from the Kilauea Volcano. We had done the Kilauea Iki Trail a couple of times, down and across a lava crater.

Miguel got tired hiking over the lava field, but I kept going, chewing up a pair of sneakers in the attempt. After about two hours I seemed no closer. I was bummed.

Miguel was very sweet and comforted me, instead of being agitated waiting for me. He said, "I have a surprise for you. I hired a couple of young natives to guide us in the morning." I was touched.

He said, "I've seen the lava up close a few times and it was no big deal to me, but I thought how I would feel if I'd never got to see it."

He did it for me, for love. I gave him a sweet and sensuous kiss and a long hug, in return. It was two hours each way, over the lava fields again. We passed by a basketball hoop sticking up out of the hardened lava.

One of the young guides said, "That's where our school used to be." Everyone chorused, "Wow!"

As we grew closer, the sneakers started getting warmer, hot even. The guide pointed down to the side where a jagged hole was opened. It glowed red down in there, and I couldn't help but think *We're walking to the gates of hell.*

Finally, as the light grew dimmer after the sunset, the smoke got closer and closer. We arrived at a cliff which fell into the ocean. The flowing lava, Pele, was sliding lazily off the edge of the cliff, less than 100' away. A plume of smoke kept rising out of the ocean as the lava poured in. I was mesmerized. It was easily the most sensational, natural phenomena I would ever see in this life.

Miguel said, "I'm glad the wind isn't blowing our way. It can be very dangerous to breathe the fumes into your lungs. It's almost like breathing in glass or cement."

Going up Mauna Kea Volcano to almost 14,000' was anticlimactic. There were many observatories from many countries. There was snow on the ground and we were cold, even with the coats we had worn. However, it was foggy up there and rainy, and the visibility was not good.

Our last excursion was very strenuous and satisfying. We did the 16 mile roundtrip, 7000' total elevation Waimanu Valley hike, camping overnight. It was crazy-steep, going on a zigzag "Z" up the cliff, crossing the raging Waimanu River twice, that runs into the ocean. Hikers have died crossing it, died having rocks fall on them, died from falling 500'.

Miguel said, "I'm proud of you. You looked like a pro back there, crossing the river, hanging onto the rope."

I said, "You know how scared I get sometimes in deep water. I had to steel myself and use my adrenaline."

Once in the valley you could count maybe a dozen sky-high waterfalls on one side, with the beach and ocean on the other. The wind began to pick up and then came the downpour. We had to go into the port-a-john to cook our food, the wind was that strong. We laughed about that later.

Miguel disappeared a couple of times for a while. He was 'helping' a poor damsel in distress who had been strong enough to do the crazy hike, but couldn't put up her own tent which did not have a cover.

He had the gaul to ask me, "Should we invite her to sleep in our tent?"

"Let her sleep in the port-a-john or ask one of the other guys camping out," I replied, without pity; "Our tent is barely big enough for two, are you serious?"

It was warm enough, she wouldn't die from getting wet. And she'd learn an important lesson about piss-poor planning. The young athletic lady was gone the next morning, leaving at first light; according to Miguel, the early riser. In place of the dozen waterfalls, there were now 20.

At the end of our hike, going around Muliwai Trail again; and going straight back up the road at a 25% *AVERAGE* grade to the Waipi'o Overlook, we were beat. Down. We dragged ourselves into the car and went through a drive-through, being famished. We were so tired we fell asleep after eating, in the fast food parking lot for a couple of hours.

When we woke up, we laughed at each other sleeping in the parking lot in the day time. We talked excitedly about all the details of our excellent adventure, congratulating each other.

———————

BACK IN THE DEEP SOUTH, I quickly began working at the new hospice job. Miguel had several luxury, lake condos that were standing empty. He would occasionally loan or rent one. I suggested paying him rent, and he agreed fairly quickly. He gave me the GF "girlfriend rate," basically I paid him about half the going rate, less if I was between jobs. I kept it in mint shape, making sure I left it as good as I got it.

About two years went by. I worked and we proceeded with our lives. It was lovely not having to drive every other weekend. The condo was maybe the nicest home I ever had, and bonus: Miguel lived just down the hill.

One day we were out, attending the opening of a local Cherokee casino in the mountains. It was so packed and the lines were so long, that Miguel said,

"Do you want to go buy a Prius?"

I stared into his eyes and said, "Really?"

He knew I had been thinking about getting a 3rd Prius. I put a lot of miles on my cars and really believed in what the Prius stood for. I had gotten the 1st generation in California, having to get a used one, since new ones were on months-long waiting lists. I'd gotten the 2nd generation in Raleigh area, getting a several thousand dollar tax credit. Now I was considering the 3rd generation.

Miguel had many luxurious, sporty, classic and serviceable vehicles. He had found a really great deal in Athens. We drove to the dealership and found a beautiful, new, green/blue metallic Prius for $20K. He promptly wrote a check for a bank transfer and had them put the title in my name. We didn't talk about any payment plan.

I was so pleased and so grateful. Although we hadn't talked about payments, I didn't want to take advantage of him. I loved him. I began to give him large sums of cash each paycheck, covering the condo and the car. I could afford it.

As mom's 75th birthday drew closer, I began putting together a big luncheon party for her at her favorite restaurant. Mom's sister Sue and brother Nate were going to drive/fly into town for the event. There would be about 40 of her closest friends and family. There would be a photographer/videographer, my old friend Sam. I designed the invitations and had them printed and mailed.

What should have been a happy day for me, was DARK. I was able to put it all aside for the sake of the special day. Hell, I kept it largely to myself for about nine months, growing my new life like a baby in the dark womb.

Meanwhile, Miguel was on his annual fishing trip. He would return home in time for the party. He would pick up and pay for the unusually beautiful, decadent and delicious: triple-chocolate, three-layer cake with sugared strawberries; shaped like a heart.

All good things must come to an end. That is Buddhism 101 in Samsara: the worldly cycle of karma, death and rebirth. Miguel had just returned from Alaska. We rendezvoused at the beautiful lake condo, making love shortly upon arrival.

Something one of his friends had said was stuck in my mind: "Are you sure he's divorced?"

I quickly and emphatically said, "Of course he's divorced," totally believing in him.

I decided in that moment to ask him directly: "Are you divorced?"

"What a strange question," he hedged.

"It's a simple question. Are you divorced: 'yes' or 'no?'"

His head dropped and he wouldn't look at me...

I broke the silence, "You're scaring me."

He shook his head 'no' slightly. My world broke into a million shards, slicing me to the core of my soul.

He tried to explain: "I served her with divorce papers, but she refused to sign them. I kept hoping she would divorce ME, over the years when she had boyfriends."

She had cheated on him the last five years of their lives together. He'd been devastated and depressed and had finally moved on after she decided to stay with her lover.

I asked, "Why did you lie to me?"

He said, "I didn't lie to you, exactly."

I said, "Well, you purposely deceived me for the past seven years, almost."

He nodded his head and got up sadly, head down, and walked down to his own condo. I was crushed and in a daze for weeks after that. I poured myself into my work.

I began plotting an escape. I would go back to India and complete a pilgrimage. It would include Nepal. I would get some Ayurvedic treatments. What about the International Yoga Festival? What about a trek in the Himalayas? I had planned to make my pilgrimage *after* retirement, now I had to turn poison into medicine. Again. I refused to let Miguel's betrayal destroy my life.

Miguel tried. He seemed to think I would get over this, as I had gotten over him giving me an STD. I thought about it. *I LOVE him, damn it. I want to be with HIM and nobody else.*

I told him, "The only way we can be together is if you *ACTUALLY* get a divorce. You can't possibly have my best interest in mind if you are married to someone else, can you?"

He agreed, and then hemmed and hawed a bit and alluded to probably getting a divorce, but no actions were taken. He said he would discuss with Mrs. F, but apparently he never did.

I can't remember ever getting an honest-to-god apology.

I worked those nine months, saving my money and planning. I quit paying on the car. There had never been a repayment agreement, neither verbal nor written. I would end up paying about half; good enough. The GF rate for the condo suddenly halved.

He said to me, "Maybe we should put something in writing about the car."

I said, "That's the least of my worries."

I feared a lot of the folks that knew Miguel would not believe me. They would want to believe that I had known he was married all along. Hell, he'd led them all to believe that he was divorced with his half truths and manipulations. Even his family didn't seem to know.

I concocted a plan with mom. I had finally told her, the first who knew anything was wrong. Miguel was invited over for a nice meal. Just as he was eating his last bite of pie, I told him,

"Mom knows you're still married." His head dropped. I continued, "Do you have any questions, Mom?"

Mom (being only four years older than Miguel) said, "You *know* how much she loves you. She wanted to be with you forever and even planned to take care of you when you were old and sick. Why did you lie to her?"

All Miguel said was, "I didn't think she would want to date me if she knew." He quickly left. He had asked me not to tell anyone he was still married.

I had thought, *The nerve of him*, but said, "Your deception is *NOT MY BURDEN to BEAR*. Eventually, everyone will know."

9. Pilgrimage, a Spiritual Travelogue

We had already planned a trip to Maine before I found out Miguel was married. I talked with his sister about the situation and decided since the tickets were already purchased, I'd go ahead and go. His family was having a reunion with all the siblings and their families. I wanted to climb Mt. Katahdin at the northern terminus of the Appalachian Trail in Maine, at Baxter State Park. I needed a win.

The two of us had backpacked about 100 miles together on the A.T. a few years ago, filling in some of the miles Pamarama and Granny had skipped over. We did the rest of the Smokies. We did the area around Fontana Dam. We sang *Rocky Top* while hiking over Rocky Top, TN; laughing and cutting up. We sheltered with a couple we made friends with through a bad storm in a broken down shelter. It leaked in the half that was barely usable. The four of us had hiked into the NOC (Nantahala Outdoor Center) and celebrated with steaks and wine.

He had been impressed that the wound bandages I had insisted he pick up, had been put to good use one evening. We hiked into a shelter for the night. A middle aged couple with two college age young men were making dinner. One of the young men, the son's buddy, suddenly sliced his hand to the bone. It was pouring blood. I quickly handed over a wound bandage and they taped his hand up. They decided to load their packs back up and get on the trail to a road, so he could go to an emergency room. They moved off quickly, with him holding his hand up in the air to slow the bleeding.

In Maine, we had a diet high in crustacea: lobster roll, whole lobster dipped in drawn butter, lobster bisque, lobster everything...Until I got to Baxter State Park. My diet then became Cliff

Bars, Mountain House dinners and iodine tablet flavored water. The reunion in Freeport was fun and we visited a lighthouse at Pemaquid Point and the LLBean flagship store with the ginormous hiking boot statue out front. We took a ferry to Monhegan Island, walking all over the picturesque, artsy town.

We almost made love, finally. We were in Millinocket, the main gateway to Baxter SP. Miguel started touching me and I quickly had an orgasm. I had missed him so much. We were kissing passionately. Then something came over me and I couldn't. I cried, once again.

We got a secluded camp spot near a river in Baxter. I was used to preparing for backpacking. This time it was easy. There were no places to stay over, on top of Mt. Katahdin. I would go up and down in one day. I prayed for good weather and strength. The trails to the top are sometimes closed, due to the often extreme weather.

Katahdin is an Indian word, meaning "greatest mountain." They consider it holy and propagate the myth of Pamola, the deity of Katahdin, who would destroy those who ventured too close.

Miguel walked with me the first couple of miles from Katahdin Stream Campground, going up gradually. The trail is 10.4 miles roundtrip from there. There is an elevation gain of 4000' within five miles. It is a strenuous climb no matter which trailhead you choose. The average time for hiking it is 8-12 hours. Miguel turned around to head back down and I continued.

I got to the first really difficult spot, of many. It was a doozy. The rock face seemed to go straight up. There were a couple of metal bars in the rock. I looked straight up and got dizzy. The rock seemed to be moving, as the clouds were blowing quickly across the sky above.

The wind was blowing 20 mph throughout most of the day, with gusts up to 30 mph. Some of the youngins were wearing tank or spaghetti strap tops with shorts. I was glad I had on proper boots with long pants and shirt and my trusty Patagonia windbreaker rain jacket with a hood. My hair was held back with a large woven and colorful headband I had gotten in Ecuador. I carried a small peak-backpack with extra water and Power Bars.

While contemplating the rock face and wondering how I was going to get up there, a young couple came up and the young lady began crying. She was scared and didn't want to go on.

Her boyfriend said, "Don't worry, Honey, we'll go back," hugging her close. They left.

A young man came along, pulled himself up with the bar as a handle, grabbed the next bar and stepped on the lower one, getting a knee up on the next level. I waited until I was alone and hoisted myself up, likewise. I was unsure if I would be able to complete, if the rest was that difficult. However, I was not going to give up easily.

There were a couple of hours of rock climbing and then hopping from boulder to boulder, some of which were loose and moved. Once at the peak, I was high; literally and figuratively. The view was to die for, 360 degrees. I asked a young lady to take a picture for me, and email. I later made that photo into a holiday card before I left on pilgrimage.

I couldn't resist hiking out a ways on Knife's Edge. It looked like the backbone of a humongous dinosaur, with the sides falling off sharply.

I didn't stay up top too long, realizing I must do everything in reverse now. For at least two hours I scrambled and slid on my butt down the mountain, meeting Carol, who was also slipping and sliding.

She looked more scared than I felt, and was going slower.

"Are you ok?" I asked.

"Maybe I will be," she replied, without looking up. We spoke to two other ladies who were barely inching along, passing them.

We went together down Abol Trail which was shorter, but more technical. It took us three hours to get down from that point. Carol picked up steam and gave me strength to finish. Miguel met us, a couple hours later then I had guesstimated.

The next day we hiked on the A.T. some more, going southward. We passed by beautiful Diecy Lake; picking and eating our fill of blueberries. We saw Carol again and got a photo together. Katahdin was the most difficult mountain I climbed—even in the Himalayas (except for the altitude), I would soon find out.

I HAD PREPARED FOR nine months for my pilgrimage. I moved all my belongings from the beautiful, luxury lake condo; over to mom's house. Miguel helped me put a little storage shed together, which was in dad's little weather-worn garage; double protection.

Fortunately, with all my long distance moves in the past, I was not attached to many possessions. I did not want to be a packrat; having cleaned out the packed basement, garage and seven overflowing closets after dad died.

Miguel helped me move with his old van, avoiding my family as much as possible. We tried a couple of times to get the old intimacy back, but I just couldn't. We were broken.

I kept quoting a phrase (by Byron Katie) in my mind:

"Just keep coming home to yourself. You are the one you've been waiting for."

I played the song by Anna Nalick: "Breathe (2 AM)", over and over: "*And breathe...Just breathe...*"

I would be taking a flight from Atlanta to Seattle to Dubai to Delhi. Miguel decided to take the flight also, from Atlanta to Seattle before heading on to Kona.

We parted ways with smiles on our faces and a couple of tears. He had told me less than a year ago that he considered me family. He talked about us sharing our sorrows and rejoicing in our accomplishments. He had even promised to take my ashes and dump them in the Ganges, if I should die before him. Now we swore friendship forever, as we were parting.

My journey started off late, with a postponed flight keeping me in Dubai overnight. I took the opportunity to take an evening tour;

seeing the famous Jumeirah Mosque, the sailboat hotel (Burj Al Arab), and the tallest building in the world: the Burj Khalifa.

Three days after departure, I finally arrived in Delhi, but my bigass Samsonite bag did *NOT*. I got to the guest house—Evergreen, $6/ night (exchange rate was about $1 = Rs. 50). I was exhausted and crashed. The sounds from the street kept waking me. The Paharganj area was more decrepit than I had remembered. It is the buffer zone between the old and new. It is a budget traveler hang-out; close to the New Delhi train station.

The next day, my Samsonite with four wheels was delivered by a very nice, helpful and attractive young man. We would become friends.

I went shopping, buying: soap, Odomos (bug repellent) and a beautiful *kameez* at Connaught Circus area. The *kameez* was Indian *khadi* style: a natural hand spun, hand woven, natural fiber cloth. It was made in the same way that Ghandi had spun cloth. I had a lovely breakfast at Saravana Bhavan.

I ran into the nice young man, Nishant, several times around Delhi. He steered me in the right direction a couple times and advised me to buy my own bus ticket, rather than get it through the somewhat sketchy Evergreen owners.

There was a romantic component to our interactions, but I resisted the urge. I had gone without sex for nine months and did not intend to start off my pilgrimage with a sexual dalliance. I was not about to even *consider* marrying a foreigner again: been there, done that! I *did* give him a sweet, hidden kiss; when taking leave.

I was surprised to find the Metro now in Delhi. They had just started working on it about the time I was there last visit. It was wonderful, fast and cheap. I took it to see the Baha'i Lotus Temple. It is marble, shaped like a lotus flower. I had a vision inside, of Mother Tara being born from a lotus, ascending out the top. It is a truly inspired work of architecture.

A nice Hare Krishna temple (Iskon) is nearby. Iskon had free toilets and cheap eats. I talked with a nice Russian young lady and her mother there.

I snuck out of Evergreen a day early, taking a bus to Haridwar. I stayed at Hotel Landmark which was cleaner and more modern and had a *PRIVATE*, hot water bath/shower *AND* free wifi. It was $10/night.

I slept in and ordered room service. I went out for the Evening Aarti, the ceremony held on the banks of the Ganges each morn and night. I met a nice young man named Kapil, who showed me around and explained the Aarti as a nightly offering and meditation, in honor of Maa Ganga—the Ganges goddess. I bought him supper. There was another surreptitious kiss under cover of night, and then another quick escape from complication. I never saw him again.

The next morning I was on a bus to Rishikesh, where the Beatles had meditated. The bus took about an hour. It is a picturesque town at the foothills of the Himalayas. There was Maa Ganga (Mother Ganges) again. There are two suspension bridges where people, motorbikes and cattle crossed over. Monkeys climbed overhead on the cables. I stayed above the Laxman Thula bridge in a women's dorm at Bunk Stay, $7/night. I rested after getting my lower bunk in order and my things in the locker.

I enjoyed pizza and a papaya lassi (sweet yogurt shake) on the rooftop restaurant of Bunk Stay, drinking in the most beautiful and inspirational view. Maa Ganga meandered throughout the valley, the suspension bridge high above. The foothills of the Himalayas surrounded the picturesque scene, with temples and yoga schools dotted close to the river.

I did a little homework on the iPad mini Miguel had given me, and found the two Singh Negi brothers nearby. They had a nice package of Ayurvedic treatments, yoga classes and daily *kirtan* devotions. I met them and signed up for 10 days of heavenly treatments; vegetarian meals included. It was $1000, a fraction of what it would have cost in the States.

I was finally feeling relaxed after my long trip, having reached a chill village on the Ganges. I decided it was time to make the Miguel break-up known to my Facebook friends.

I made sure to write on my own page and didn't even mention his name. All the people who mattered, knew about our relationship, in the old high school town.

I said, "Ladies, beware. I found out my boyfriend of almost 7 years has deceived me and is married. Consider yourselves forewarned."

I announced my pilgrimage to India and Nepal and began posting photos, documenting my travels.

Many of my FB friends offered condolences and great surprise at the turn of events. Another old school teacher called Miguel a 'cad.' One of his closest friends apologized, saying they had not realized that I didn't know he was married.

Miguel's reaction was to say, "You ruined my reputation."

I said, "No, *YOU* ruined your reputation."

———————◉———————

THE NEXT TWO WEEKS were glorious. After the early morning devotions/kirtan, I would drink pure ghee (clarified butter) and hot water only. My treatments consisted of: a full body massage daily for over an hour, and then warm oil dripped on my forehead for half an hour. I would emerge two hours later with my oiled hair wrapped up in a towel. My special vegetarian lunch was presented shortly, on the pleasant patio.

I would then go to the guesthouse, have a warm shower and nap and return for supper and sometimes yoga and evening devotions. I could hear the evening Aarti going on at the riverbank. I felt compelled to share that I was a Buddhist, as the devotions were usually related to Hinduism; Shiva in particular.

The eldest Singh Negi brother said, "All Buddhists are Hindu."

That made a lot of sense when I thought about it: Jesus was a Jew and Buddha Shakyamuni must have grown up in a Hindu family.

I decided to leave Bunk Stay after I got my laundry back and my favorite black leggings were missing. I refused to pay the laundry bill. I showed the young man at the desk the list I had made of laundry items.

There was another reason I decided to hightail it. A young German woman was now staying in the women's bunk room. She seemed very nice and sincere, practicing her meditation. But one night, I was rudely awakened by a couple of strong jabs or pokes.

I startled awake, saying, "What the fuck?"

The German lady said rudely, "You were snoring."

I said, "That's not really something I can control. It's certainly *not* a reason to put your hands on me."

I was not able to sleep the rest of the night. A group came in during the night and I decided to get up at first light. I packed as quickly as I could and left a little "gift" for the German woman. Her cosmetics were all over the tiny bathroom, taking up all the small counter space that everyone shared. I put the smelly brown gift inside her face powder jar, from the stopped up toilet.

It was not one of my better moments. I was learning to deal with my anger and I knew that had been an action of pure anger and spite. I was ashamed of myself but also, secretly amused. I never told a soul that nasty tale and hoped I hadn't made the lady sick. I determined to purify my mind and soul and to be a better person. I would work on snuffing out the *Three Poisons: Ignorance, Anger and Attachment.*

I moved farther away, up in the Tapovan area, to Hotel Nature Villa—maybe two miles away. I met a lovely Russian lady, Tamara, who was taking massage classes. She made a comforting cup of chai for me with her electric teapot. We had the bunk room all to ourselves for a couple of days.

I continued to enjoy the Ayurvedic treatments. There were some different treatments added: a bundle of herbs that were spanked all over my backside and then roughly rubbed in. I inhaled steam of an herbal potion under a tent of blankets. I was given some herbal medicine which gave me diarrhea for a day or so. Oil was put in my nose.

I had read that it was important to have the long life Ayurvedic treatments before age 60. I never completely understood the ancient medical system, but began to feel more energized. I would be ready and purged before beginning the International Yoga Festival.

I met wonderfully interesting people: young ladies from Australia, Ukraine and Austria. I had lunch and tea with Mica from Austria, overlooking Maa Ganga. They were staying at the Vedic center with the Negis; studying meditation and yoga. A wonderful sadhu played a flute at one of the kirtans. At the guesthouse I enjoyed some of the tunes from my iPad with a nice Argentinian lady who knew many of the words and sang with me.

One evening the youngest Negi brother gave me a lift on his motorbike up to Tapovan. Another day it had started raining and an old man stopped and gave me a ride to the Vedic center on his motorbike.

I developed a cold and a bee stung me. I realized I was purifying and kept up my treatments, yoga and devotions.

I had my last treatment and said goodbye to the lovely Singh Negi family. They said I could use their address and/or phone number if I needed to while I was in India. I had breakfast with my Russian friend Tamara and then began rolling Bigass Samson on the four wheels towards Parmarth Niketan Ashram, on the other end of Rishikesh. It was very large, with something like 2000 beds, positioned on the River Ganges near the other suspension bridge, Ram Jhula.

The room was heavenly after the bunkhouses: only two beds and a private bath with hot water. Purified water was in each hallway to drink. I bought a Snickers candy bar and a Coke Zero to celebrate my 57th birthday. On returning, a new roomie had arrived: Natalia from Australia. She said her mother was Aussie and father was Sri Lankan.

She had many colorful tattoos which I admired. I showed her the one on the small of my back: the colorful lotus flower I'd gotten in SoCal with my 4th ex, back in my early 40's. That was before everyone else in the USA got tattoos. I had decided I would be happy with it even if I lived to be 100.

The next week was a whirlwind of yoga classes, various teachings and a couple of concerts. Each morning and evening was an Aarti on Maa Ganga riverbank. I packed in as much as I could, reveling in the active spiritual vibe of the place and event. I was out early and back late. There were ~26 offerings per day, impossible to do it all.

People from 93 countries of the world were there. I happened to sit with a Canadian and a Mexican for lunch in one of the huge food tents. I joked, "All of North America is represented."

I rarely felt lonely while in India and least of all at the IYF. I met Neeta from Calcutta who gave me cough medicine, Amira from Singapore who gave me cold medicine, the soulful yogi George, the nice and famous Indian yogi Dr. T.A. Krishnan who was staying down the hall...

I forgot one morning, dashing out of the food tent with my coffee and three of the delicious small bananas. A monkey bounced off me and snatched half my bananas. Startled, I went into defense mode, kicking another large monkey soundly, yelling "No!"

They took off and a young man was laughing at me. I began to laugh too, until a young lady scolded me,

"That's why you're not supposed to take food out of the tent."

"My bad," I replied ruefully.

At one of the evening Aartis, I sailed a little boat made of half a coconut shell, incense, a lit candle and flowers out on the river; making the offering and saying prayers for everyone's happiness. I was very moved. A new friend, Mikey, helped me up and down the slippery steps to the river.

I was baptized the second time in the Ganges, performing ablutions in the cold river. Hindus believe Maa Ganga is a goddess and they worship her. It is believed she washes all your sins away, purifying you for the next life.

I loved trying out the different styles of yoga: ashtanga (very physical) with Mark Roberds, somatics yoga, kundalini yoga with Gloria Latham and Gurmukh. I was thrilled that I was able to keep up, even in the high energy classes. I realized I was definitely an intermediate level yogi.

There was SO MUCH: The teachings by Sri Mooji and Sri Prem Baba; HH Swami Ramdevji and HH Drikung Kyabgon Chetsang (Buddhist); the love of HH Pujya Swami Chidanand Saraswatiji who was the spiritual head of the ashram...One day I walked in front of him without realizing, swiftly apologizing with a namaskar (greeting with hands in prayer position).

I said, "I'm sorry."

He gently touched my cheek, looking with love into my eyes, and saying: "Don't worry," bringing tears to my eyes.

———◉———

THE TIME HAD COME TO proceed towards the first pilgrimage stop. I had purified with Ayurvedic treatments and a week of intense yoga. I felt ready and very enthusiastic as I took a taxi back to Haridwar, and then a train from Haridwar to Bodh Gaya. While in the taxi I saw an elephant alongside the road, very auspicious.

I caught up on my emails and FB, thanking everyone for birthday greetings and posted photos. I wished Miguel "Happy birthday." He was headed to Munich to visit friends and he did not want to FaceTime. He sounded a little lost, but maybe that was wishful thinking.

I got on the crowded Doon Express train, having to force my way between a couple of guys, wielding my Bigass Sam as a missile. I fought my way through the crowd, finally getting to my lower berth where an old guy and two older ladies were stowed away. I had to almost rudely ask them to move when I got too tired to sit up. I finally was able to recline after locking Bigass Sam to one of the bars on the window with my cable. It didn't even bother me anymore that one of the ladies and the old man sat at my feet and head, on the edge of the berth.

Bigass Sam was now missing one of his four wheels. I would use him as a safe when I'd go out on a town, locking him to a heavy metal bed or a sink pipe. It had a combination lock and the hinges were on the inside.

My backpack was about all I needed, usually. It had a padded section for the iPad. It had a couple of locking sections and theft-proof straps with metal mesh in them. One of the pockets had RFID technology, to keep electronic credit card info from being stolen.

The next morning, much of the crowd had gotten off and I made friends with a young mother, Subha, and her son in the berth across from me. I found out that the train was running about three hours late and I would arrive in Bodh Gaya well after midnight.

I was on the train about 20 hours. *Wallahs* would come on to sell their food and drinks: chai, two eggs with rice and broth, chips, bananas, bottled water. It was just cool enough, with the window open. I had habituated myself to the smells of curry, grease, urine and other unknown smells.

I finally arrived at my stop at Gaya and haggled with the *tuk tuk* (auto rickshaw) drivers to take me to Bodh Gaya. It was much longer than I had thought, and I gave a nice tip to make up for the paltry sum Subha had told me to bargain for.

I slept late at Beauty Guesthouse, past noon; showered and got ready to go to the Mahabodhi Temple. It was the Highest Holy Day (Holi) and the full moon was rising. It was the Display of Miracles Day in Buddha Land. It was a most auspicious day to begin my pilgrimage. I was filled with gratefulness and other spiritual emotion as I walked onto the grounds, seeing the temple below and in the distance, for the first time. A nice Japanese man took my picture for me at the entrance. I slowly walked down the stairs, and took in all the stupas and offerings of flower garlands and Buddhist flags. I walked reverently into the temple and bowed to the yellow sandstone statue of the Buddha, encased in glass. I bow, not because the buddhas require it, but to show respect and to humble myself.

I walked around the temple and *THERE IT WAS: THE TREE*. The bodhi tree under which the Buddha attained enlightenment. Overcome with emotion, I sat down abruptly. I wept with joy.

I did a circumambulation and then spread out my yoga towel to do my meditations in earnest. I knew that according to Vinaya text, *Treasure of Quotations and Logic*, "All actions done on this one of four special days are magnified by 100 million times!" On those special holy days every meditation, every circumambulation, every mantra, every mandala, every prostration was multiplied. On top of that, being in such a holy place would also be a multiplier. I did not waste any time.

There were many monks and nuns and people from all over the world. I finally felt like I had arrived at my place in the world. I felt at one with the space and pilgrims. I could die happy here.

Buddhist lore says that if you go to Bodh Gaya, the place where the Buddha attained enlightenment, you go towards the path of enlightenment in all your future lifetimes. If you do not reach enlightenment within Shakyamuni Buddha's era, you will be a foremost disciple of future Buddha Maitreya.

The next day was also one of the holy days and most of the town was shut down. I found a hotel restaurant (Mallika) that was open and had the continental breakfast: mango juice, toast, two fried eggs and black coffee; Rs. 200. I caught up on my emails, uploaded a couple of pics and notified FB friends I would be on a silent retreat for the next week.

I did a full range of meditations back at Mahabodhi Temple. I saw a beautiful South Korean monk in traditional gray hanbok and said,

"Annyonghaseyo," bowing. He appeared astonished that an American woman in Bodh Gaya was speaking with him in Korean, and smiled so that his eyes crinkled.

While in meditation on my yoga towel, the wind began to blow gently, and then briskly. Some of the holy bodhi leaves began to waft down to the ground. One beautiful heart-shaped leaf fell in my lap! I ran after another leaf nearby, snatching it out of the air, giggling. I put them in my meditation journal. Every time the wind blew, *THE TREE* would gift a few bodhi leaves. Monks, nuns, small children and old people would all run after them and laugh, competing a bit with one another to catch them first.

The tree trunk is blockaded off, but its many big branches extend over, high up. There are big metal column supports under some of the heavy branches. The seat at the foot of the tree is in the blockaded area. You can see it. It is a slab made from red sandstone at King Ashoka's direction. It is considered: 'The navel of the Earth; The Diamond (or Vajra) Throne'. It is where the Buddha sat in meditation; cross-legged for 49 days until he became enlightened. <u>The cover of this book has a photo I made of the holy tree in India, with my iPad.</u>

The Mahabodhi Temple Complex is almost 12 acres. It was recognized as a UNESCO World Heritage site in 2002. The temple is a pyramidal tower, 180' high. It has four smaller towers at the corners.

At supper I met a nice looking man, Michael from Toronto. He told me about His Holiness (HH) the Karmapa and receiving teachings from him, as a disciple. The Karmapa was in town and I would have an audience with him before I left Bodh Gaya.

I registered for a silent retreat at ROOT Institute in Bodh Gaya before I left the States. It is a small monastery compound connected to the Dalai Lama, with mostly western patrons. I went and was assigned a private room, simple but comfortable. The bathrooms were just around the corner outside, one western style and one eastern style.

I did not take part in many of the teachings and meditations that week, but remembered us talking about 'pilgrimage' and how pilgrimage is an act of renunciation. That made a lot of sense, already. Nothing and no one would come between me and Pilgrimage.

I knew I would not have been welcome if they knew I was now a disciple of Venerable Geshla Kelsang Gyatso Rinpoche. My reason for being there was to go with the group to access lesser known pilgrimage sites that are located around the area. I met some very nice pilgrims that I would keep in contact with for years.

The group was permitted upstairs in Mahabodhi Temple to see the inner shrine/gompa. We made light offerings by the lake, lighting 100 candles to join the maybe million candles already burning after sunset. We did a walking meditation, chanting "Om Mani Padme Hum," twirling the many (152 total) prayer wheels.

The next day we went to Nalanda University ruins and Vulture's Peak at Rajagriha, where the Buddha had given many teachings. It still felt like a campus with its tree lined walkways. That area was where the Buddha had expounded on the Heart Sutra, the Prajnaparamita Sutra, and had given the 'Flower Sermon.' We were joyful, walking the hills where the Buddha had walked.

I enjoyed a short meditation in Vishwa Shanti Stupa (World Peace Stupa). My former Buddhist practice with the Japanese Soka Gakkai was connected with that beautiful and peaceful place on Ratnagiri Hill.

The next day we went to Satarparni Caves and meditated, making some light offerings. The Buddha had meditated in those caves and they were located near where the first Buddhist Council had met in 400 BCE.

Next day we did a nice hike up to Mahakala Cave where the Buddha had practiced austerities. We drove by Sujata Temple where the Buddha accepted milk-rice from Sujata under the Banyan tree. It was nice and windy, with a lot of Buddhist flags blowing. A leaf presented itself to me and it went inside the meditation journal with the others.

One of my Buddhist nun friends would later design and make a most beautiful stained glass with leaves from the holy trees embedded in the glass.

On the last day, we went to Gurupada Cave on Mt. Gurpa where Mahakasyapa has been meditating in equipoise, inside the mountain the last 2500 years. He is waiting for the coming of Buddha Maitreya, the future buddha. It was 1680 steps up to the top. *Wowza.* There was a beautiful altar in the bosom at the top of the mountain, wedged-in. We pilgrims hung prayer flags on top of the mountain. It was nice and cool, with a drizzle of rain.

After the retreat, I went back to Beauty Guest House. Another clothing item was sacrificed to the laundry, at ROOT Institute this time. I was taking everything much more in stride now, feeling generous and compassionate. I prayed, *May everyone have beautiful clothes to wear.*

I went to Mahabodhi Temple daily for meditations, and then to Be Happy Cafe for lunch. A train ticket was bought for Varanasi.

I DECIDED TO GO TO Tergar Monastery (where the Karmapa School of Tibetan Buddhism is) where the Karmapa was giving audience to individuals who signed up. It was to be three and a half hours until my time slot, so I had jasmine green tea, chips and Mountain Dew. I found a cool spot in the temple banquet hall. It was empty and I was able to take a little nap in a hidden nook. A banner on the wall said, "The 8th Khoryug Conference on Environmental Protection for Tibetan Buddhist Monasteries and Nunneries in the Himalayas." It was a lovely, huge room with a huge Buddha statue.

I went on the spur of the moment, realizing it would probably be my only opportunity. I had no *kata* (Tibetan prayer scarf) to offer, no envelope for money to offer. I decided I would bow and give Rs. 500, hoping it would be private. I had thought a lot about what I wanted to ask the Karmapa.

It was finally time to line up. A long line went around the room a few times and up some stairs. I finally got to the top and it was my turn. I barely had time to do one prostration, putting my forehead on the floor, and offering Rs. 500. An attendant came up behind me and one in front waved me up, listening to the side a bit. His Holiness, the Karmapa was standing and I had to look up.

I said to the Karmapa, "I can ask anything?"

He nodded his head and appeared to be listening intently.

I asked, "Will you please help to heal the rift in the Buddhist community between HH Dalai Lama group and Venerable Geshe Kelsang Gyatso group in your lifetime?"

He looked away and then stepped up close; popping his eyes, crazy-like, semi-threateningly at me. I did not move, only gazing into his eyes with compassion and earnestness and great hope.

His facial expression changed and he replied, "That's a very difficult situation!"

I said, "Please think about it. It's a very big problem."

He agreed to think about it and nodded.

I bowed my head with a namaskar, saying, "Thank you."

I was given a lineage mandala with the Karmapa's handprints in miniature in red, stamped on it; a blessed/protective, red string bracelet and a packet of spiritual medicine pills. I was shaking as I left, tears in my eyes. I was relieved I had had the courage to stand my ground. I was also relieved I hadn't been thrown out.

HH Karmapa is the head of the Karma Kagyu, the largest sub-school of the Kagyu, itself one of the four major schools of Tibetan Buddhism. He is seen as the most influential Tibetan Buddhist religious leader after the Dalai Lama. The Karmapa lineage is the most ancient tulku lineage in Tibetan Buddhism, predating the Dalai Lama lineage by more than two centuries. A very informative book was written by Mick Brown: *The Dance of 17 Lives; The Incredible True Story of Tibet's 17th Karmapa.* I happened upon it one day, and read it with great interest; some time before any preparation for pilgrimage began.

I had just met HH 17th Karmapa, Ogyen Trinley Dorje. He knew something about legitimacy, having gone through intrigue when he was recognized; and also the Chinese recognized their own Karmapa, trying to control the Tibetan Buddhists. That was highly unusual since the Chinese government is secular and has previously denied reincarnation.

A year later I found and read the Karmapa's 'Special message of truth, courage and great humility,' on his website. There was also a posting about Dorje Shugden, the dharma protector who had been denigrated. It appeared that the Karmapa, dealing with his own legitimacy at the hands of the Chinese government, was taking seriously the rift in the larger Buddhist community. I wept with gratitude.

I meditated for four more days at Mahabodhi Temple. One day a Nepali-Bhutanese nun offered me fruit. We meditated side by side. It was getting hotter by the day, up to 100 degrees one day.

<hr>

I TOOK THE HWH-JSM Express from Gaya Junction to Varanasi Junction. The train was more pleasant, less crowded than the last. I had a lot of snacks and drinks while chatting with some of the passengers, including a French guy.

Varanasi is an ancient city. It was called Benares and also Kashi, in earlier times. It is the spiritual heart of India. Many Hindu, Jain and Buddhist (and others) attend the many temples and are baptized in Maa Ganga.

Once in Varanasi, I took a bike rickshaw into the narrow alleyway maze to Hotel Alka, Rs. 850/night. I was in a tiny room with a very high ceiling. The roof restaurant was just outside my door and the tiny little shower/toilet rooms were just around the corner. It was hotter, getting up to 110 degrees in the afternoon. I slept late that first day, getting up to walk to Manikarnika (burning ghat).

Legend has it that Lord Shiva dropped an earring into a pit at Manikarnika. It is considered the center of the five tirthas, the navel of the universe. Tirtha is a holy place, but it has a more esoteric meaning. It is a channel, where the spirit world and the human world intersects.

I understood those places as the 24 Holy Places of Heruka and Vajrayogini; very powerful energy centers—where Dakas and Dakinis would come to bless Tantric practitioners. I felt the energy of Varanasi could be one of those ancient places; or perhaps it was one of the Charnel Grounds—the most fearsome and abhorrent places (filled with corpses, skulls, fire...).

I spent about two hours meditating on death, watching the public cremations going on continuously outside, on the bank of the Ganges. There were six or seven cremations going on while I observed.

Sanjay, a nice young man became my unofficial guide. He said, "More than 27 cremations can be done at once." He showed me big stacks of different kinds of wood for sale, to burn on the pyres. Banyan was the cheapest, mango was mid-price and sandalwood was the most expensive.

The bodies were covered with silk cloth and dipped in the Ganges to purify them. Male family members were the pall bearers. The oldest male shaved his head except for one lock in back, dressed in white, and lit the funeral pyre.

It was very efficient, taking about three hours to completely burn a body. What was left was only the hipbone (woman) or thigh bone (man), and they were tossed into the Ganges. I watched a dog wade in and come back out with one of the large bones.

I read an article in an Indian newspaper about how electric crematoriums are beginning to gain popularity. They are cheaper and faster and less pollution goes into the thick air.

The next day I hired Sanjay's little brother to take me out on a little boat. He rowed me up and down the Ganges so I could see the *ghats* (four miles of big concrete steps going into the river; lined with temples and shrines). The ghats are multi-purpose: laundry is spread on them to dry, snacks are sold on them, gatherings for various purposes... I ended up back at Manikarnika for further meditation, closer this time.

I watched a male body (white shroud) brought in, face uncovered for a moment. More wood was piled on the body. Sandalwood dust chips and pure ghee (butter) was poured on top. The family person in white went to the eternal fire that has been steadily burning for 3500 years, caught a bundle of long grass on fire in that Shiva flame, and went down to light the pyre.

Sanjay put some ashes on my forehead from the eternal fire; as an Indian tikka mark, saying a short prayer of blessing. The photo on the back cover of this book is from that experience.

I opted to give a donation to a hospice for poor people for a cremation. I opted out of other 'donation' opportunities and declined going to Sanjay's mother's silk shop. I enjoyed decent spaghetti back at Hotel Alka. I could hear the Aarti nearby, further down the river, with many boatloads attending.

One of my favorite restaurants was Dosa Cafe. I got the masala dosa—a huge savory crepe with two dipping sauces. For dessert, I had the choice truffle *idle* with ice cream, both fermented. Idle is a type of cake made out of fermented beans and rice. The restaurant had only three tables, all of which stayed full. It was recommended by *Lonely Planet Guide India* (by Sarina Singh, Michael Benanav, Abigail Blasi, Paul Clammer, Mark Elliott, Paul Harding, Anirban Mahapatra, John Noble, Raub and Kevin Pages).

Another favorite place was Blue Lassi, also recommended by *Lonely Planet Guide*. It had been open for almost 100 years, staying in the same family. It is in the alley maze. I ordered a delicious chocolate and pomegranate lassi. I sat on the cement bench, watching the foot traffic go by.

THE ADVENTURES OF A SOUTHERN BUDDHIST

The alleyways are so narrow a car can't drive through, but motorbikes and an occasional cow go by. I got quite lost once and grew weary walking so long in the heat. I asked a young man with a baby for directions, and he gave me a ride back to Hotel Alka on his motorbike, which was nearby.

A funeral procession went by with horns and drums and the pall bearers carrying a corpse on a pallet over their heads. They were headed to the burning ghat.

I hired a driver from a nearby hotel to take me to Sarnath for a few hours (Rs. 40). Sarnath was where the Buddha first taught. I got up early that morning and had breakfast on the rooftop with a Korean man I had met the day before. He was retired, having owned a *hogwan*, like the one I had worked at in Korea.

Sarnath was cooler, with a nice breeze blowing and a lot of nice shade trees. I saw everything: three stupas, a museum, a bodhi tree. I meditated for a while in the shade of the main Stupa, Dhamekh. It was beautiful. The museum held many Buddhist relics uncovered during excavation, including Ashoka's Lion Capital, in excellent shape. The grounds were beautiful with lots of flowers. The driver was very nice and patient.

It has been said that if you go to Sarnath, the place where the Buddha first taught/preached, the dharma will penetrate deeply into your mind. You will be able to teach/share dharma and further its growth.

I was halfway done with my pilgrimage and was ready to leave hotter'n hell Varanasi. I used my iPad to reserve a room at the Linh Son Vietnamese Chinese Buddhist Temple in Kushinagar, which was further north and close to the Nepal border. It was where the Buddha died and attained *paranirvana*. That is when you attain nirvana after death; it is a release from Samsara, karma and rebirth.

While checking my email and posting on FB, I saw that my tax refund had been deposited. I played an April Fool's joke on Miguel: I told him, "I've taken a job and will be staying in India."

"Congratulations," said the quick email back, "is it a social work job?"

I washed my clothes in the sink and hung them around the room. I had my usual cheese tomato toast, bananas and coffee for breakfast. I ran into the French guy I had met on the train. He was headed for Sarnath.

———◦———

I GOT ON THE OVERNIGHT bus to Gorakhpur (Rs. 350), arriving before light after six and a half hours, struggling to find the next bus to Kushinagar. It was packed. I finally got an uncomfortable seat, slept a bit with my head on Bigass Sam, another hour and a half. A short tuk tuk ride and I was in Kushinagar. The gate to the Vietnamese temple was locked, so I went across the street to an open air chai stand. I had a couple cups of chai, chatting a bit with the nice owner. An hour later, the gate keeper came out and gave me a room.

I unpacked, showered and slept until after noon. I went to the Yama Cafe next door for lunch, having nice egg noodles and a small bottle of orange soda. I took pictures of the Vietnamese and the golden Burmese temple behind it. I then walked about a mile to Mahaparanirvana Temple, where the Buddha died. It was about 97 degrees, not well over 100 degrees as in Varanasi.

I was a bit dispirited that there were several druggie types skulking about, and even the government appointed gatekeepers asking for tips, coming and going.

There was a sign up that said: "Give no donations."

I pointed to the sign and insisted, "I am not a tourist; I am a pilgrim, a Buddhist."

Now, I tried to have a couple of bills on me so I could give alms when asked. That's what the Buddha and Jesus expected, if you could. I tried to give, with wisdom.

The grounds were very interesting, with several stupas and ruins and a nice bell. Inside the temple, I wept. The Buddha statue was lying on his right side, depicting death. It was beautiful and very sad. I circumambulated and then sat in the corner, doing my meditations.

It has been said in Buddhist lore, that if you go to Kushinagar, where the Buddha died, you will increase your lifespan. You will not die with fear or anxiety. You will be able to create the causes to have control over your death and rebirth.

I met several nice people that week: a nice Nepalese woman, a Chinese man, some children who begged there. I really enjoyed chatting with Mr. Roy, who owned Yama Cafe.

It was Hindu New Year when I went to Rambhar Cremation Stupa, where the Buddha was cremated. There was a carnival/picnic atmosphere, but I was able to meditate a bit. There was a nice breeze and it was still cool. I saw an ancient buddha statue.

One of the monks told me, "I knew you were Buddhist by the concentration lines between your eyes. You are from the Sakya tribe."

The monk set up a motorcycle ride to get me back 'home,' on the Meditation Garden shortcut, which was pleasantly shaded.

Yama Cafe was closed next day, due to New Year's. I went directly to meditate and make prostrations while it was still cool. After, I got a bike rickshaw to an ATM a ways off, since much was still closed. Using the ATMs was so much easier than travelers checks had been, last time I was in India. My Discover Card did not charge an extra fee for international ATMs as many did.

On the way home, I stopped at Government Buddha Museum, Rs. 10. It was small but very interesting, similar to the one at Sarnath.

Back at the Vietnamese temple lodging, I paid Rs. 2400 for the six nights I had stayed. I realized my filter water bottle had disappeared. I'd had it last at an outdoor cafe.

Pilgrimage was 3/4 done. I would take the bus back to Gorakhpur and then on to the border town of Sunauli. I used my iPad to arrange three nights in Lumbini; over the border into Nepal; the last official pilgrimage stop. It was $68 and included breakfast each morn.

Meanwhile, I rested in the main, cool meditation room at the Vietnamese temple with the fans going. I was appreciating solitude more and more. I realized that it was because my monkey brain suffered when presented with endless distractions and dramas. I picked up easily, the thoughts and emotions of those around me. Peace of mind was becoming more priceless as time went on.

Just as I was meditating on solitude, a precious puppy came and joined me. Then a group of Indian tourists/pilgrims came in and began taking photos, wanting me to be in them; so much for solitude.

I did my laundry in the sink and had one last meal at Yama Cafe; thukpa noodles with veggies and an orange Fanta. After, I had a last chai at my favorite outdoor cafe across the street. I would miss little Kushinagar, population 13,000+. I spoke with the resident monk at the Vietnamese/Chinese temple and found out he was from Michigan and had last lived in Orange County, CA. He was Asian-American.

———◉———

IT TOOK THREE AND A half hours on two buses to get to Sunauli. After a sweet and a soda at a shop, I got my passport stamped to leave at the border. I changed my INR (Indian rupees) to NR (Nepali rupees) to save time and make it easier.

However, at the Nepal crossing they insisted I go back and change NR to dollars; which included another exchange fee. I felt like I was being taken advantage of and wondered if I should continue. I sat down in the station and argued with the nice young man.

"What do you mean? You won't take your own currency? I just paid to have my INR changed into NR to make it easier."

He was pleasant, but firm. He wouldn't budge.

He said, "It's regulation."

I sat there almost two hours. It was one of those international moments when it was just too much. I was tired after the long bus ride and rolling the now three-legged suitcase another mile in the heat.

Finally, I observed a young Israeli couple arrive. They were given the same command and they quickly went back out and then returned with the accepted currency.

Something clicked for me. I realized this was not important in the grand scheme of a pilgrimage. I would dedicate the wasted money and the frustrated tears for Great Enlightenment for ALL Sentient Beings throughout the three times.

I apologized to the young man: "I'm sorry. Thank you for being so patient. I realize you're only doing your job. Thank you for the chai."

Within half an hour I was checking into a border hotel, NR800; with private bath and wifi. Just as I settled down for a nap, the power went off. Without the ceiling fan it got pretty toasty. I went down for dinner: cheese omelette, fries and lassi.

The next day after two short and crowded bus rides, I arrived at Hotel Ananda Inn, which was very close to the main gate of the Maya Devi complex. In the morning I became excited again. I had a whole other country to explore and my pilgrimage was shiny and new again. It didn't even bother me too much, when I realized I'd left the iPad charger at the border hotel. I borrowed one from the attendant and handed over a bag of laundry to be done.

It was NR200 to get into the Maya Devi complex, for the Lumbini Development Trust. There was a long walk down a tree lined road. There were lots of people all around. A big three-day festival was going on. Too bad, not a great time to do serious meditation.

At the Maya Devi Temple, a guard assisted foreigners into the back entrance to see the spot where the Baby Buddha had been born. It was in a big building with a catwalk going all the way around. It was built over the open ground. The spot where Baby Buddha was born was right at a big flat boulder area. There were ruins from 3rd century, BC to 7th century, AD. There were all kinds of offerings there: flowers, coins and

Buddhist flags. I prostrated and again felt the rush of gratefulness and love well up.

I went back around the catwalk where pilgrims were lined up and found a semi-secluded spot to meditate.

Buddhist lore says that if you go to Lumbini, where the Buddha was born, you will create the karma to have control of your own rebirth; to be born in pleasant places with good circumstances.

Outside, there was an ancient Ashoka Pillar and a large bodhi tree with prayer flags flying all over. There to the side was the tank where Buddha's mother had bathed after the birth. I went down the slippery steps and promptly busted my ass again. I had fallen at my hotel on the slippery marble steps that had been mopped, with no signage.

I slid halfway into the water with the turtles and laughed. Nearby was a very nice monk in a wheelchair. He twirled a prayer wheel in his right hand. His head and body were deformed, but his personality was delightful. His English was very good, like many Nepalese. He said he got polio as a child and was nearly blind. I left him with NR50, after seeing others give him money.

I had fried chicken pieces and a Coke Zero for lunch outside the grounds. Back at Hotel Ananda I had banana crepes and coffee. I mused that Nepal seemed nicer than India so far, but a bit more expensive. The hotel was a treat with excellent hot water and a western toilet with a bidet. The new tv was nice and big, and the bed had a softer mattress than most of the very firm beds I had slept on so far. There were TWO sheets and a real bedspread, unlike the rest with only one sheet and a big plush blanket. The desk and closet were other pluses.

The next day I walked around and looked at a lot of other temples from various Buddhist groups and countries. The German Temple was especially striking with its bold and colorful paintings. There were nice walks by a canal with trees lining the path on both sides.

I had veggie *momos* (dumplings) for lunch, and found a new

charger for my iPad for $5. It had an Indian/Nepali style plug, so I wouldn't have to use my converter.

On the third and last day I meditated at Maya Devi after the free breakfast. I felt a huge sense of accomplishment, but no welling up of emotion. I thought, *maybe I have grown. It's not about the emotion, after all.* I had completed my pilgrimage, visiting and meditating at the four main places Lord Buddha Shakyamuni had graced with his presence.

Each amazing place had it's own flavor and feeling. The pilgrimage had required a couple of very long train rides and quite a few bus rides to navigate between the four sites. It had even required crossing from India into Nepal. The hardships were offered to the Buddhas of the three times.

I was even grateful for Miguel. Because of his betrayal, I was here now. When I'd found out he had never gotten a divorce, I was so distraught that I had to make a big change. Breaking up with the love of my life had given me the impetus I needed to turn poison into medicine.

I had done what I set out to do; out of love and devotion for the Buddhas, myself and all sentient beings. I prayed that they would all reach full and perfect Enlightenment ASAP. I thanked the Buddhas of the 10 directions, and left with a grateful heart. *Namaste.*

Back at my hotel, I contemplated going on a bonus trek. I would go to Kathmandu, Pokhara and then on the Annapurna Circuit through Muktinath. I already had 500 miles of the Appalachian Trail under my boots, I could do it. I would save Dharamshala, Ladakh, and other places for another time; preferring to remain a pilgrim, and not a tourist.

10. Annapurna Circuit, a Spiritual Adventure Travelogue

The Paschim Nepal Bus to Kathmandu took off a bit after 5:00 a.m. The first toilet stop was in the woods. The ladies went one way and the gents another. We had passed several perfectly good public toilets. About five hours in, a big landslide stopped us short. It was in a godforsaken area on the mountain with nothing around. The men began shoveling and it was extremely dusty. The one nice thing was the river down below and a nice mountain view beyond.

I borrowed a nice Chinese lady's umbrella to have a bit of privacy, peeing in semi-public. There was nothing else to be done. I felt fortunate that my hotel had packed my breakfast for the journey. I shared the sammich and egg with the nice Chinese lady, she shared her banana and apple. I had also brought along pizza, not knowing I would have a packed lunch. I saved the chocolate and chips for later. I had plenty of water and a Coke Zero, but only sipped, not wanting to have to pee again on the side of the road.

A cute Chinese guy said, "It's Nepal New Year."

"Happy(f'n) New Year," I said. I was relieved to be fairly patient with the long delay. There was nothing else to do but fan and talk a bit and read. We finally arrived in Kathmandu just after dark.

I got a taxi to Hotel Lovely. It was a nice room with a soft bed AND a sofa. The private, hot-water shower and good internet were a relief after the exhausting, prolonged trip. It began to rain, hard. I went to the rooftop to enjoy the cool, refreshing rain. I had a good night's sleep and awoke to a nice cool day. The hotel cafe had delicious, filtered coffee.

The next couple of days were a whirlwind of activity. Boudhanath Stupa was fantabulous and full of positive energy. It, along with

Swayambhunath Stupa, is an example of mammoth Buddhist architecture. They are some of the oldest burial monuments in the world.

The area around the perimeter of the humongous stupa felt very cosmopolitan. There were people/pilgrims from all over the world. The restaurants were quite varied, and I tried many of them.

I joined in the *Kora*, the circumambulation around the stupa. I turned each of the 655 prayer wheels around the perimeter, which sent more than four million prayers out to the universe. My prayer beads counted off the mantras I chanted. The air was full of a continuous loop song/chant:

"Om Mani Padme Hum, om mani padme hum,
Om mani padme hum, om mani padme hum."

I find myself to this day, singing that tune. It is lilting and lively and positive. I was still singing a Shiva tune from Rishikesh, as well.

My favorite restaurant was Kori's Korean Restaurant. The food was great and the view was to die for. I watched the flocks of pigeons and flocks of people walking around the stupa. The Buddha eyes of the gigantic stupa looked at me joyfully. A little boy stopped to feed the pigeons. A huge vat that reminded me of a witch's cauldron coughed out clouds of incense smoke. It looked like a circular courtyard with the stupa in the center and the shops and restaurants on the circumference. It felt like a Pure Land to me.

Sitting on a park bench looking at the Buddha Eyes on the stupa, I meditated. A nice, good looking Hungarian guy sat down.

He said, "My father died while I was volunteering in the Himalayas. I was at different monasteries, training monks on how to work out."

I said, "I happen to be a hospice social worker. Tell me more."

Death and dying were old friends to me, and I talked with him for almost two hours. He was flying home the next morning for the funeral.

THE ADVENTURES OF A SOUTHERN BUDDHIST

Supper was lovely Vietnamese pho (noodle/veggie/tofu) and a Vietnamese coffee, chilled. I finally finished my laundry which had been soaking in the large bathing bucket for almost two days. I caught up on FB and wrote reply email messages to mom, Miguel, Nate and others. I found an ATM and prepared for the next day at Kathmandu Durbar Square.

Kathmandu Durbar Square is very historical and ancient. It is at the heart of the ancient city of Kathmandu; a complex of beautiful temples and shrines, Hindu and Buddhist. Most of the shrines are built in the pagoda style, between the 12th and the 18th centuries. The kings were crowned there. It is one of three royal palace squares; all of which are UNESCO Sites.

It still had a lot of earthquake damage. The various temples and buildings were in various states of repair. It was disconcerting. I sat at Himalaya Coffee and enjoyed watching the view and the people passing. A beautiful Nepal national flag was blowing nearby.

I happened onto a little golden, metal cage house that was open, and entered. It turned out to be where the Kumari Devi was sitting! The Kumari Devi is thought to be a living buddha. She is a pre-pubescent girl, very beautiful. She was called Kumari Unika VajraCharya.

I was very surprised, blurting out, "Are you the Kumari?"

The young Kumari said, "Yes," with a lovely smile.

I said, "Nice to see you," with a namaskar and a bow.

The Kumari said, "Same to you," with a beatific smile.

I backed out quickly. The unexpected encounter had been thrilling but shocking. I had been unprepared, but felt blessed and loved.

Back at Boudhanath, I enjoyed tuna sushi and miso at Sakura. I sat at a window overlooking the stupa. A beautiful Japanese lantern hung in the open window.

I enjoyed two massages and a facial at Harmony Spa, in the area, during that week. They were very affordable and needed, after all the

3rd world travel and trekking. Another awesome meal was had at La Casita Spanish Tapas, also overlooking the stupa. The Mediterranean salad with seared tuna and frappe was very satisfying to the tastebuds.

The next kora session was in the lovely rain with my green Patagonia rain jacket; then a lovely fish meal at the hotel. The next day I slept in and then played on my iPad while waiting for what appeared as a humongous chicken club burger. I would take part of it and a margherita pizza with me on the bus to Pokhara.

It was a nice ride with interesting people to talk with. The nice middle-age Bulgarian-German lady beside me flirted with a young man in front. Just before dark, the bus arrived in Pokhara. The hotel was good enough with wifi, warm water, but no restaurant. There was a nice view in the distance of the mountains.

There *was* the nice Hallal Restaurant and Roti next door. They cooked bread in a Pakistani style oven, slapping the dough on the wall of the open flame cooker. The chicken tikka was superb.

The next day I began preparing for my trek. I went for my ACAP permit and TIMS (Trekkers Info Management System) at Nepal Tourism Board. They were NR2000 each. Each trekker had a duty to check in at each check post on the Annapurna Circuit.

Three years before, about 30 persons died at the pass on the Annapurna Circuit. A blizzard had blown in suddenly and they froze to death trying to find the covered trail. If they had stayed together at the teahouse or even huddled together in any semi-shelter, they might have lived.

Everyone I talked with thought I was a bit crazy to be trekking alone in the Himalayas. I hoped that all my backpacking skills on the Appalachian Trail would keep me safe. I had studied all the little guides I could find, mostly online, making notes.

A working ATM was found (3rd try), and then lunch with a nice view of Phewa Lake. The grilled fish and latte were satisfying.

I relaxed and supplied for my trek a bit: pack cover, water treatment tablets, BPA-free water bottle; all for $14. It came a torrential downpour after the dinner with a lovely traditional Nepalese music show with dancers. The new pack cover worked pretty well after adjusting the top better. Trusty green Patagonia was still awesomely dry. It rained so hard that the roads became like small rivers, and I walked past the side street to the guesthouse, having to backtrack.

I stopped and talked with Tenzin at a nice Buddhist shop. We talked a bit about the various Buddhist deities and he asked, "What is your Buddhist name? Who is your guru?" I reveled in the conversation, happy to be in a country with so many Buddhists. We also discussed trekking in the Himalayas.

I told him, "I trekked 500 miles in the mountains with my mother, in the USA."

He said, "Then you can do," with a namaskar.

On the following morn, I walked the other way out of the side street, to Fujiyama Japanese Restaurant overlooking Lake Phewa. I had a filling fish broth, chicken soup; coconut lassi and brewed coffee. I bought more protein bars for the trek. At a coffee shop I enjoyed a fun band that evening. The chicken cheeseburger and fries tasted really good, but I woke up that night with a tummy ache.

Diarrhea took its place and I had to call the front desk at Hotel Diplomat. The nice young man brought me up more toilet paper, asking if I needed medicine.

I postponed the trek. After taking anti-diarrheal medication three times, I began to feel better. I wasn't able to eat until the next evening, having a banana and protein bar with a lot of Emergen-C powder. I slept most of the day and all night, becoming stiff and sore from the hard mattress.

I finally got out the next day, squaring away the bill with the hotel and walking in the hot sun to find an ATM. Back at the hotel I was feeling weak and broke into a sweat. I took a nap. When I woke up I began packing my small backpack. I kept it very light, as there would be guesthouses to eat and sleep in on the AC trek. I took bigass Sam down to the reception area for the owner's family to keep for me until I returned.

The lovely owner of Hotel Diplomat bought a bus ticket for me to Besi Sahar, the first check post I would enter.

He said, "I give you ride," pointing to his motorcycle.

On the way to the bus stop, he pointed, saying, "Look!" I caught my first real glimpse of some bigass peaks: Fishtail (Machhapuchhre—22,943') and Annapurna South (23,684'). The sun was shining on the peaks that were towering over the layer of clouds below. They looked impossibly high.

The Himalayas are about 1500 miles long and 150-200 miles wide. Their average height is about 20,000'.

———————●———————

I SAT BY AN OLDER, nice Japanese guy on the crowded bus. Also on board was Casey, a Japanese-American guy who liked to talk a lot; Stuart from the UK who had been living in Thailand, etc.

The bus stopped for lunch and several of the passengers began talking about the AC and their plans.

One guy asked, "Do any of you want to hire a Jeep together to go further up in the mountains?"

I listened to several guys agree on a Jeep, and decided I could afford to go with them to Jagat (NR 1500), a little further up in the mountains. It was a torturous ride that bounced us poor passengers around like ping pong balls as we hit each pothole. I thought I might pee myself several times during the two and a half hours of bruising jolts.

We were SO happy to reach Jagat and get another stamp on our AC passports and check in to a guesthouse. New Mountain House was NR 100, with wifi. I had pizza and Fanta for NR 620, with a free breakfast lined up. The room was *very* basic, with twin single beds, a little table and a trashcan; but the view was to die for. There was a rushing river running through the green canyon with houses on the hill across the way, nestled into the mountains. I settled in for a long rest and caught up on my email.

The Annapurna Circuit is one of the many available treks in the northern part of India and Nepal; in the foothills and mountains of the Himalayas. I had considered the Mt. Everest Basecamp trek, having a hankering to see Mt. Everest.

However, after much research, I had decided on the AC, wishing to experience Muktinath—a holy place just over the three miles high pass at Thorong La.

The classic Annapurna Circuit trek was 130 miles. Many trekkers added to that or did a shorter trek by beginning higher up in the mountains, or by ending at various towns on the downside of the mountains.

I would do almost 75 miles in 13 days; hiking about five and a half miles per day. In addition, I would stay in Muktinath several days. I would take Tara Air from my end point at Jomsom, back to Pokhara. Then Buddha Air would fly me back to Kathmandu; from where I would fly back home. I loved that the airlines were named after buddhas, and thought: *Nepal is my new favorite country*.

It helped me to make my decision when I realized there were more guesthouses along the way and the AC was not nearly as frequented as the Everest Basecamp trek. If one promised to eat at the same guesthouse where one slept, there was a considerable savings.

The Nepalese Rupee went about a third further than the Indian Rupee. That was good, since the further one went up into the isolated mountains, the more expensive everything got. I did not begrudge the Nepalese folk this, because they had to bring everything up, Up, UP at great discomfort and expense.

I had learned to travel light and only had my small peak backpack with the security features; besides the clothes and hiking shoes on my back/feet, and the one trekking pole I had finally bought on sale while backpacking on the Appalachian Trail.

I had my silk long johns, hiking shirt and pants, cashmere sweater, down jacket and windbreaker rain jacket. I slept in a silk sack which was super lightweight, as was everything else. I had an extra town t-shirt and several pairs of wool socks and undies. I had treated most of my outdoor clothing with Permethrin to avoid bed bugs and mosquitos.

I carried a water bottle and a few snacks; my notes and maps and journal. My trusty iPad was ready to take amazing photos and email when the guesthouses had internet (not infrequently; but maybe just in the dining room).

One of my sources online that I Googled had been particularly helpful: *Trekking the Annapurna Circuit, Including new NATT Trails which Avoid the Road by Andrees de Ruiter and Prem Rai.*

I had been surprised that my pepper spray and old pocketknife had made it unquestioned past all security on the way from the USA, packed in and checked with bigass Sam.

I swore to myself to take it easy and acclimatize, as I was hiking at a higher elevation than ever before. I loved adventure, but only took calculated risks. Severe altitude sickness is a real thing and when it hits, one must get to a lower elevation ASAP or perhaps die. While trekking, other hikers and I would murmur about the helicopters that came down off the higher mountains. They were most likely rescuing a young, fearless male who had hiked too far, too high, too fast.

<hr/>

ON DAY ONE OF THE TREK, I went from the little village of Jagat to the little village of Tal. In between, there weren't many people. The views were getting better and better. Every river crossing involved a suspension bridge. It began raining and I could see snow on the higher elevations.

Peaceful Guesthouse had an awesome hot water shower, and I

washed out my undies and cashmere. The fried *momos* were very tasty and the apple pie was bigger than a pot pie, easily big enough for two. A huge pot of tea helped take the chill off the room while I recharged the iPad and posted some photos.

One of my favorite photos was walking the AC through a village, a waterfall very high up ahead, a horse standing on the steps of a house, head in the door. I took the time to order mom a dozen red roses (her fave) for her birthday, online.

Day Two of trekking included about 1500' of elevation, to about 7000', in the village of Danaque. There were beautiful waterfalls along the way and I ran into Casey from the Jeep ride. Lodging was at Motherland Hotel—nice, but rather neglectful of guests. It took some time to get the hot shower working, apparently the gas had run out. Next was a long wait for a pizza. It was cold in there. They kept opening the door and leaving it open when they'd come in the dining room. Shivering, I shut it.

The walls were very thin and I heard a couple of Asian young ladies chatting for some time, like they were in the same room. It took me a while to get to sleep, so I slept in a bit the next morning.

I had discovered some hemorrhoids, most likely due to the elevation. There was an embarrassing exchange when I made it to a shop that had medications.

I asked the young lady, "Do you have medicine for hemorrhoids?"

She said, "What?"

I repeated, "Do you have medication for hemorrhoids?" She didn't get the word "hemorrhoids."

The young lady laughed when I pointed to my backside and mimed/said, "Swollen."

"Piles! Piles!" She said, pealing with laughter. I ruefully laughed with her. The medication, Pilex, *did help* shrink them. I also purchased a new charger for NR 500, as the new one had already died.

Day Three of trekking had a lot of uphill. I fell in with a group of middle-aged to old folks. They showed me a little shortcut and suddenly, I caught up with the Asian young ladies and a French threesome.

The clouds dissipated and I caught an eyeful: Manaslu Mountain, 26,781'. With a smile, I soaked it in. At Temang village I took the trail instead of the road, meeting a Boston guy and his daughters again. When the trail became vertical, I went back to the road, losing about an hour. The deodar cedar forest was very fragrant and the nice farms were very soothing to look at.

I passed the Asian young ladies again after putting my Cho-Pats on my aching knees. As I walked into the village of Koto, I saw a sign for *momos* and while waiting for them, played with the cutest little girl who enjoyed 'peekaboo' behind a curtain and enjoyed zipping/unzipping my jacket.

I was very tired when I walked to the edge of Chame and got my passport stamped at the checkpoint. The lady of a guesthouse waylaid me, Peaceful Guesthouse (popular name). I took a long hot shower and enjoyed supper and conversation with a nice German man, Michael. The tuna macaroni with brown sauce was delicious after trekking all day. I washed out my clothes and laid down for a nap.

There was no internet, but the view more than made up for it: Annapurna II. It was snow covered and gigantic—26,046' high.

———————⬥———————

DAY FOUR, I WAS FEELING good. I love backpacking and this was turning out to be easier than the Appalachian Trail. The Annapurna Circuit is marked well and it runs through a village every few miles. Some are tiny, but others are more sizable, with more choices of guesthouses and restaurants.

I began passing others I had seen on earlier days. I had the feeling that maybe I had lived in these mountains in a past life, like I was home. I felt that the Buddhas were definitely looking out for me. On this auspicious day, I viewed both the Annapurnas II and IV, and also Pisang Peak. I came right to the foot of a bowl shaped mountain called Swarga Dwari (Gateway to Heaven).

I stopped at an apple orchard and had two very sweet apples and a Sprite for the road. I ran into Stuart who was now with two Russians. I talked with the two young Asian ladies; they were from Ho Chi Minh, Vietnam. They had hired a guide AND a porter, who was humping a *humongous* load, about the size and shape of a small piano box.

I beat them all up the mountain to Dhukhur Pokhari, which was a little shy of lower Pisang. I had already gotten a room and was eating a tasty tuna macaroni and sipping ginger/honey/lemon tea. It began raining and I watched through the dining room window as the others trudged by below, heading to either upper or lower Pisang.

It was cold in the guesthouse, but I ordered some hot soup for my room. The new cable was charging nicely. I was excited that I was now over 10,000'. I reminded myself to take Ibuprofen daily now, until I got over the pass, at least.

Day Five, after an early breakfast, it began raining lightly as I left the guesthouse. The rain turned into snow by Lower Pisang. I considered taking a jeep a ways with some others at the restaurant, but there were too many people. I decided to trek in the snow a while. It continued to snow, but I was on the road and never felt unsafe. I managed to stay mostly dry and warm; only my socks/shoes/gloves were wet.

I passed four or five hikers and then caught up and passed the Vietnamese ladies again. I got a room at Gandhi Hotel along the way, in Humde village. I sat in the kitchen on a bench, facing the open fire, with two young ladies from Spain. They had also attended the International Yoga Festival in Rishikesh, and we compared notes.

The nice lady of the house made me a delicious thukpa: vegetable noodle soup. I then took a good and warm shower in the little shack outside by the road. It seemed to be heated by the fire from the kitchen, with pipes running there. After a nice nap, I caught up on email and FB photos in the cold room. Supper was again at the kitchen fire: tuna and cheese momos and ginger/honey/lemon tea.

Day Six was short by design. There was still snow on the ground, but it was a beautiful clear-blue sky day with snowcaps on the peaks. Michael from Germany happened by and told me of a monastery nearby. I hiked there, but it was locked. It was 900 years old. On the way to Brak(g)a, I passed a sign for Milarepa's Cave. Milarepa was an infamous, storied Buddhist monk for the ages. I hoped to hike up there on the next day, but it wasn't to be, this trek.

The next guesthouse had a lovely room in what looked like a western style mountain cabin, and food for $27. There was a lovely view of one of the Annapurnas—I thought IV or even III, but the lady at the desk said II. The freshly washed red hiking shirt, yoga/hiking pants and undies were flapping in the breeze, in good company with the Tibetan/ Nepali prayer flags.

I was served at a lone table outside with another truly once in a lifetime view. There was a small river running along below the mountains. Looking up, uP, UP you could see the Annapurna snow peak high above; the intense blue sky giving a sharp contrast. As the wind blew, you could see snow blowing off the peak, up towards the bright sun.

Although I had given up beef and pork, I occasionally had some 'wild' meat. I decided I needed some meat to get up to the pass. It was a first: a delicious yak burger with yak cheese, tomato, onion, carrot, lettuce, mustard; on a freshly baked bun. It came with lots of fries. It was one of the best and most memorable meals on the AC. It was huge and juicy and I savored.

In the bakery, the smells were heavenly. I could not resist the brownies and chocolate cake. Yum. I didn't eat much sugar stateside, but while trekking at high altitude, the calories were needed for energy. The clothes dried very quickly and l was left with a bit of a sunburn on my face from the hour enjoyed outside at lunch, sans hat. I took two Advil and drank lots of water. The elevation was now over 11,000'.

I woke up that night, feeling like I couldn't breathe, after dreaming of being trapped. It didn't help that the covers weighed a ton and my boyfriend had betrayed me. It felt something like an elephant sitting on my chest.

I reminded myself out loud, "It's the elevation." I decided then and there that I wouldn't make it to Milarepa's Cave, although I really wanted to. My priority was making the pass and Muktinath. I would walk shorter distances each day as the elevation got higher, avoiding altitude sickness.

On Day Seven, I made the hike short—to Manang, taking me five hours. It was a nice set-up at Hotel Yeti, similar to the last, but with a solar shower. I fueled up on a salad, cheese omelette, cheese toast and strong coffee. Back in my room, I washed out my undies. I could hear the wind howling outside and made a mental note to wear my windbreaker tomorrow.

After resting and eating, I spent my time listening to podcasts and editing photos until dinner: a mouth-watering chicken sizzling platter with fries and cabbage veggies. I got to bed a little early. I was getting a little better at high-altitude sleeping: keep cooler, keep head up more, NO restrictions on neck or chest; more water and Ibuprofen.

ON DAY EIGHT, I WAS feeling great. I got packed before the brunch of garlic soup and chocolate brownie with coffee. Heading uphill I met the lovely Ram, a Nepalese Buddhist. He was about Clay's age and was very interesting to talk with. I can't remember our conversation, but he felt like an old friend (maybe from a past life). Of course, trekking at those altitudes prohibits long talks.

He was headed to a hotel he owned up the mountain and we began trekking together to Yak Kharka. He had an even smaller pack than I did and only wore a t-shirt.

We stopped for tea and visited with one of his friends on the way. She was also a guesthouse owner, and they talked business.

We made great time and got to his hotel as it began snowing again. I got the last room at a bargain rate. The snow was really coming down. I enjoyed watching it and the cattle moving past the window on the trail, while eating the mixed macaroni with lots of cheese. Yum.

We had passed several, including young Israeli woman again, three couples and another lady. I enjoyed talking with Ram and his family, showing them the photos of my pilgrimage and trek thus far. We parted with a namaskar as I went to bed.

On Day Nine, I made it short—a climb of 1308' to Thorung Phedi. I was now at 14,551'. It was sunny and snow was not a problem, although a bit slippery and cold. Again, I passed most of the others who had left before me. I arrived there in three hours, feeling fine.

My room had no heat again, but with attached bath (cold water) and more light. I changed out of wet clothes, hanging them up to dry.

I was still tripping after going through the 'Landslide Area.' The signage had warnings, such as:

'Danger! Landslide area. Do not stop, do not walk close together, walk lightly, walk quickly. Look for falling rock.'

I took the warnings to heart and set off at a steady pace, about 20' behind a lone young man. I paid close attention to the trail, being careful not to stumble or dislodge stones. I glanced up the crazy-high mountain to my left occasionally. There was a steep drop-off to the right.

Shortly, I detected a quick movement and an unknown sound. I saw a shadow and ducked, as a boulder the size of my head whizzed past. It fell with the velocity of a cannonball, almost exactly at the midpoint between me and the young man. We watched as it crashed down past us and kept going.

He had turned and we stared into each other's eyes. His face was white and his mouth was open, mirroring my own, I'm sure.

He said, "That rock was as big as my head!"

I said, "That is exactly what I was thinking."

If the boulder had struck one of us, we would most likely have been dead. It fell so fast, from so high up and was so large...And if we had been walking abreast, it would have taken us both down the mountain.

We quickly finished the next mile, in silence and with trepidation. Once we had completed the landslide area, we exchanged information. The young man was Tyler from Florida.

He said, "I'm writing an adventure blog and will write about the boulder incident." I said silent prayers of thanksgiving for our protection.

The restaurant at the guesthouse was warmed by solar heat. I took the liberty of closing the windows and kept an eagle eye on the door, making sure it stayed shut. The organic Nepalese coffee was delicious and the pizza was quite tasty.

It was a groovy scene, with a couple-dozen backpackers relaxing and talking about the upcoming pass. I recognized about half of them.

Pulling out my iPad and notebook/journal, I began double checking the route and decided on a hike/climb of 1308' again, the next day. It would put me up to 15,859' and High Camp. It was the last stop before the most difficult climb—my bid for Thorong La Pass. That would be more than three miles high, being the highest point on the Annapurna Circuit.

As I drifted off in the cold room, under the feather bed and with my down jacket on; my thoughts turned to the 30 some who had died at the pass three years before. I prayerfully recited Buddhist mantras to make my mind peaceful.

The next morning, I took my time at breakfast, thoroughly enjoying the fried eggs and the cinnamon roll that was as big as my face. The coffee was exceptional.

IT WAS A HARD CLIMB on Day Ten, but I made it. It was a beautiful sunny day. I stayed at Thorong High Camp View Hotel & Restaurant. My room was very basic, and the toilet was outside in the snow and ice. Many of the same backpackers were again in the solar heated dining room: the nice German couple, Stuart (British teacher in Thailand), Grace from Vietnam, older man from France...there was a very positive vibe.

Having paid the NR 250 for wifi and NR 100 for electricity to charge, I answered emails from mom and Miguel and FB friends. The garlic soup and honey/ginger/lemon tea were comforting. Garlic and ginger supposedly helps with the altitude. Later I had fried eggs and french fries for supper and went to bed early. Tomorrow was the big day. I determined to be up by 5:00 a.m. and begin my ascent at 6:00.

My sleep was fitful that night. It was bitter cold and my tummy was upset and hurting. I took two anti-diarrheal tablets preemptively, drinking lots of treated water and then more. I had on two pair of socks, two shirts, my down jacket, gloves and the large headband from Ecuador. I added long johns and my windbreaker in the morning.

As I headed out the next morning, on Day Eleven, the sun came up slowly over the bigass mountains; appearing exaggerated, like a caricature. It was a beautiful day with a blue-black sky. The sky got darker and darker blue as the altitude increased on the AC. The scenery was very wintery and I had to wade through the snow at times.

It was entertaining to watch the older French guy try to get a horse ride about half the way up. Three guys got on three small horses, and the horses refused to budge. The guys had to get off.

I kept passing people slowly, pausing often to catch my breath. Finally, I could see a bunch of prayer flags high up where the people looked small. I got to the top at about 10:00 a.m. I was elated, laughing and chatting with those at the **Thorong La Pass, 17,769 feet high.** A nice man took my photo with my iPad at the pass, with all the prayer flags and the official sign of commemoration and congratulation.

A small tea hut was nearby, but I had already decided I would not be staying on the pass for very long. It had been about 2000' to the top. It would be about 4000' down to the first guesthouse: Hotel Paradise and Restaurant at Chamber Bhu, just inside Mustang. It had a lovely view of Muktinath Valley. That is one of the few areas in the world where Tibetan Culture still survives in its original form. It is inside the Tibetan Plateau; the "Roof of the World."

I read the book, *The Dance of 17 Lives* (Brown), about the Karmapa again when I returned home. He had escaped from Tibet and the Chinese government over the Thorong La pass in the *WINTER*, and made it down to Manang; headed east on the Annapurna Circuit, staying in a trekkers' guesthouse. They had hired a helicopter that came from Jomsom and then headed towards Kathmandu. I would always have that deeper connection now, after having been in the same magical places where my gurus had overcome their *maras* (demons).

I limped the last 1000-2000' down. My right knee was really hurting. I got a room and napped; after eating some *thukhpa (*meat, veggie and noodle dish), Tibetan butter tea and then rhubarb tea.

I woke up to the sound of voices on the other side of the thin wall. It was Stuart and Grace. Stuart knocked on my door, having figured out from the owner that I was there.

He told me, "We were delayed by an accident. An Indian man fell off the mountain a ways and broke his leg(s) and messed up his face. It is possible he also broke other bones and had a concussion."

Grace continued, "We went back to tea house at the pass to call for helicopter. The helicopter could not go to rescue, because weather turning snowy and foggy. Then we went down to here to ask for help, hot tea and blankets. The rescuers come from Jomson and go on foot and bring man down on a board."

I sat there with my mouth open, and said, "Wow. Wow—that could have been any of us. You guys are awesome. That man is so fortunate; what a story to tell."

I SLEPT WELL THAT NIGHT, having arrived at a lower elevation than the day before. I said a prayer for the broken man. A breakfast of veggie momos and sea buckthorn juice and coffee livened me up after my long recovery sleep. Stuart and Grace joined me at the end of the meal and we packed up and headed down the mountain to Muktinath together. It was 1300' down. We arrived in less than two hours on another bright, sunny, gorgeous day. The views demanded stops for photo ops.

Going inside the back gate of the Muktinath Temple grounds, we first came to the Padmasambhava Temple with the 8th century statue Padmasambhava had made of himself. I made three prostrations, with my forehead on the floor. I made a donation, out of gratitude for my successful pilgrimage, and also being grateful to be able to visit such a historical and spiritual place. It was a simple, lovely old temple. I asked a nun, "Please show me Padmasambhava's footprints," pointing at my feet.

She showed me Padmasambhava's *knee* prints embedded in stone, pointing to her knees. I would never have found them on my own. They were in an obscure place in the now arid brush, to the west of Thorong La pass.

We saw a couple of men in underwear or bathing suits. That was *highly* unusual in India and Nepal, and especially in a traditional Buddhist/Hindu compound. We went down the hill and I saw one of the sights I'd pined for: there were the 108 faucets, shaped like boar's heads. Spring water was gushing out of each one. 108 is the number of beads on a prayer mala (rosary).

Stuart, who was not religious, began stripping down promptly and said, "I'm going!"

He started around the circle, being baptized under each fountain of water. He was imitating the Indian and Nepalese men ahead of him. Grace took a little video.

I told Grace, "I'm going too—please video!"

I would also be baptized. I was very warm from hiking and the sun was shining. I began to strip down: off came the long-sleeved red hiking shirt, the yoga pants and two pair of socks. What was left was the black silk long johns; a pair of green Hanes panties and wool trekking bra underneath. I pulled on a short sleeve black t-shirt for good measure, and off I went.

That water was COLD. I went as fast as I could, dunking my head under each spout. Grace took the video. There were two pools at the end, and I jumped after Stuart into each one.

Being overcome with gratitude for my life, pilgrimage and faith; I kept saying, "Thank you. Thank you," to the Buddhas. My prayers continued with several mantras. Taking my water bottle, I filled it up with a little water from each of the springs' spouts.

Back in dry clothes, we viewed two small temples, both Hindu. Leaving that area we saw two large prayer wheels, bigger than myself, hydro-powered. To my left was a large Buddha with half a dozen sadhus (Hindu religious men; wandering ascetics from various traditions).

As we three backpackers headed into the little town, I had a huge smile on my face, due to a sense of accomplishment, satisfaction and just plain fun.

We had lunch together at Hotel Bob Marley. Taking my sweet time, I savored the salad and apple/cinnamon tea (NR 500). While we were eating on the deck, a most vivid and auspicious rainbow presented itself—quite the good omen. After lunch we walked back towards the Muktinath temple and got rooms at The Paths of Dream guesthouse, NR 300 plus food.

I luxuriated in a hot shower and then washed half of my trekking clothes. I had to wait for them to dry before washing the others. The room was bright with two big windows; with awesome views of the mountains.

At supper, a dozen young Russians filled most of the dining room.

Grace and Stuart arrived later. The wifi was working and I caught up family and friends, more or less. I mused (for years) how I could ever properly explain the enormity of the pilgrimage and trek.

Once again, I was fortunate to be at a most auspicious temple for the multiplier days. It was a Buddhist holy time: *Saka Dawa*. As usual, I didn't waste any time doing my meditations at the temple complex.

At the Jwala Mai Buddhist Gompa, the two grates were practically hidden in an ancient temple that looked more like a little house. They were at floor level and you had to lean over to see the two small flames, one with water surrounding it. There had been three flames originally, but one had finally gone out some years ago. They were reputedly natural and perpetual, burning without help from humans. I had read all about them in the short book/pamphlet entitled: *Muktinath, Secret Treasure of Annapurna...The Rainbow Bridge* by Susan M. Griffith-Jones.

The temple was dedicated to Buddha Vajrayogini practitioners, due to the fire element. There was a large painting on the wall, of Vajrayogini in union with her consort Heruka. 20 nuns, the Jyomos, look after the small temple. It has been said that they are Dakinis. Being a Vajrayogini tantric practitioner, I felt a close kinship. I felt so fortunate to belong to a religious faith that has powerful female deities. My hair, still mostly dark brown, was waist length. I had grown it out to look like Vajrayogini.

In truth: after viewing, praying and meditating at the Muktinath temple complex; I felt like I planted a wonderful piece of myself there, in Muktinath. Muktinath (or Muktitirtha) is considered a thirtha; a place where the bridge between the different realms is present. It truly did feel as if a mandala had been opened and remained. Part of me would always long to return to the Muktinath Valley.

I meditated on the ancient teaching *The Heart Sutra, The Heart of the Profound Perfection of Transcendent Wisdom: "Form is emptiness; Emptiness is form."* I contemplated the rainbow and the hologram as form dissolved into space, or emptiness.

I recited the Prajnaparamita (female wisdom Buddha) mantra: "Gate', gate', paragate', para-samgate', bodhi svaha."

I had read several translations, but really liked: "Gone, gone, gone beyond, completely gone beyond. Awake! So be it!"

I returned the next day, Buddha's Birthday, and performed my meditations with gladness in my heart and a joyful mind. Nothing would ever be the same for me again. Now I could die happy, and without regret, having completed a meaningful life.

I felt whole again. I would never again feel dependent on a man for my happiness. I could love all, with compassion; and without unnecessary attachments.

I had solved the meaning of my life and was at peace. I would turn everything in my remaining life into The Path. I was on my way to becoming a *bodhisattva* (a person who is able to reach nirvana but delays, out of compassion, in order to save suffering beings). I knew my Enlightenment was ensured. I would 'wake-up' like the Awakened One, the Enlightened One. I would be truly **Woke.** I laughed out loud.

NOT THE END ;)

Author's disclaimer:

This work depicts actual events in the life of the author as truthfully as recollection permits. Author has also referred to many notes, journals and emails. While all persons within are actual individuals, most names and some identifying characteristics have been changed to respect their privacy.

Don't miss out!

Visit the website below and you can sign up to receive emails whenever Pamela McConnell, MSW, LCSW publishes a new book. There's no charge and no obligation.

https://books2read.com/r/B-A-JMRU-TGIAC

BOOKS 2 READ

Connecting independent readers to independent writers.

About the Author

Pamela McConnell, MSW, LCSW was raised in a fundamentalist/evangelical Christian church and family. At age 34 she converted formally to Buddhism. She has recently completed a Pilgrimage in India and Nepal. Earlier, she spent two years in Asia: a year teaching English in S. Korea and a year in Pakistan with her 3rd husband.

She worked as a counselor after earning a B.S. in Psychology. She worked as a hospice social worker for the last 20 years of her career after earning an MSW degree and becoming licensed as an LCSW.

She is an avid backpacker and trekker, having done 500 miles on the Appalachian Trail and more than half of the Annapurna Circuit in the Himalayas.

She may be reached at: pammyprius@gmail.com.

Ingram Content Group UK Ltd.
Milton Keynes UK
UKHW040723080323
418175UK00004B/404

9 798201 601713